THE
EICHMANN
KOMMANDOS

by Michael A. Musmanno

MACRAE SMITH COMPANY : PHILADELPHIA

FOREWORD

DURING THE PERIOD IN WHICH CAPTAIN (JUDGE) MUSMANNO, U. S. Navy, served in Germany, I was first deputy and then Military Governor of the United States Zone of Occupation in Germany. As the trials of the war criminals were under my jurisdiction, I kept in close touch with them with the aid of a legal staff headed by Charles Fahy, a former Solicitor General of the United States.

Much has been written about the Nuremberg Trials, their legal basis, and their proper status in history. While military government was not responsible for the conduct of the trials which were conducted before the International Military Tribunal except for the final approval of the sentences, it was responsible for the subsequent trials undertaken before our own courts in the United States Zone of Occupation. Even the review power of the Allied Control Council was meaningless, as the sentences of the International Military Tribunal could be changed only by unanimous agreement.

Perhaps this had some bearing on our decision to proceed with additional trials before our own courts in our zone of occupation, as it was the original intent for all of the trials to be conducted before the International Military Tribunal. Certainly, Soviet participation in the International Military Tribunal had not been received happily in the nations of the world where justice prevails.

Thus, in our zone of occupation we proceeded not only with the trials of those individuals indicted for specific war crimes, but also with the prosecution of twelve group trials selected in an effort to cover the range of German political and economic life which seemed to have contributed without duress to the aggressive policies of the Hitler government.

These cases included certain individual combines, the physicians and surgeons who used political prisoners for

7

experimental purposes; the Storm Troop leadership which carried out the mass murders; the military leaders who had exploited occupied territories; the Justice Ministry which had violated all normal concepts of justice in condoning mass extermination; and the Foreign Office experts who had worked to create the international situation in which aggressive war promised ultimate success. While not all of these trials resulted in convictions, those which dealt with acts of atrocity were proved by overwhelming and incontrovertible evidence. Among these cases was the Einsatzgruppen Trial before a court of which Judge Musmanno was the presiding judge, and which he now describes from the record with which he is intimately acquainted.

Every effort was made to conduct these trials in solemn dignity under the recognized rules of law governing the submission of evidence and with a high sense of justice. It was essential that a complete record be made available to convince the German people of the relentless cruelty of the Nazi regime and the grasping rapacity of its leaders. Moreover, if such events were not to occur again, their full nature needed to be a matter of record.

It was my responsibility also to serve as final reviewing officer for the approval of the findings and sentences of the courts in our zone of occupation. Here again, before final action, a careful review was made of the record to be sure that there was neither miscarriage of justice nor conviction based on evidence not normally accepted in a court of law. It was my view then and it is my view now that it was only through the record established under accepted rules of evidence before the International Military Tribunal and in our own courts that the true story of Nazi infamy was demonstrated to the German people and to the world. Moreover, if these trials had not been held some of the most ruthless murderers in the history of the world might well have escaped any penalty for their crimes.

foreword continued

I do not believe that the German people should be held forever responsible for the Hitler regime, but it is important to re-examine the record now and then, particularly as the passage of time permits us to consider it with reasonable objectivity and while the story can be told by living participants in, or witnesses to, the history of the time.

The story which Judge Musmanno tells proves once again the wisdom of the Nuremberg trials. Perhaps in its retelling we will find the inspiration to renew our faith in the democratic processes and realize once again the threat which any dictatorship poses to the safety of the peoples of the world. Unless we do occasionally re-examine the record, I fear we would soon refuse to believe that men and governments could have been so cruel.

GENERAL LUCIUS D. CLAY

PART ONE

The Court

PART TWO

The Indictment

PART THREE

The Modus Operandi

PART FOUR

The Trial

PART FIVE

The Verdict

Fourteen officers of the SS (Elite Guard) were sentenced today to hang for at least a million killings. The sentences wound up the biggest murder trial in history.
The men were leaders of the "Einsatz Kommandos" . . . special extermination squads sent . . . to do away with peoples classified by the Nazis as racially undesirable.

NUREMBERG, APRIL 10 (1948)—(ASSOCIATED PRESS)

PART ONE

The Court

CHAPTER ONE

IT WAS IN JANUARY, 1946, THAT I FIRST SAW NUREMBERG. I knew it had suffered terrible war damage but I was not prepared to find it stark with ruin and desolation. However, as I walked the broken streets, the gaunt and mutilated buildings on either side still revealing some of their original classic beauty, I wondered what Nuremberg must have been before the first Allied bombers made their appearance in the blue-enameled sky.

Although I preferred to think of Nuremberg still further back—before the Nazis had started it on its moral decay—I kept visualizing it during the days of the spectacular Hitler rallies with which, during the previous ten years, it had become mostly identified. Suddenly, in reverie, I pictured myself in the midst of one of those boisterous celebrations, the streets filling with cheering, vociferous crowds as military tanks clanked and brass bands blared over the storied cobblestones. I could see swastika banners writhing and snapping from every elevation. Resounding drums filled the air with gymnastic clatter while human robots, in resplendent uniforms and iron hats, kicked high their unjointed legs as they puffed by reviewing stands aglitter with brass, gold braid and marshals' batons.

14

Parades, processions and singing throngs converged on the vast Nuremberg Stadium, its towering concrete peristyle aflame with flags and bunting. The four-hundred-yard colonnade stretching across the forward end of the field seemed a dike to contain the sea of humanity sweeping in like a tidal wave. The amphitheatrical concrete piers stood as palisades to hold in check the three hundred thousand jubilating, shouting zealots of Nazidom. Silver bugles pierced through the cacophony—and presently the bedlam ceased like lungs suddenly deprived of air.

In precise geometrical files the three hundred thousand turned into statues, their right arms outstretched in stiff salute as down the center aisle, a third of a mile long, one man moved. Snare drums softly but acutely rolled a continuing homage as the solitary figure advanced toward the lofty podium. Measuredly he mounted the spiraling steps, and presently, standing on the high, wide platform like a captain on the bridge of his ship, he surveyed the frozen human ocean before him. For a moment all was still as a panoramic photograph. And then the atmosphere burst apart with a three hundred thousand throated savage cry of devotion to the death: "Heil Hitler!" The massed voices were as a roar of hungry lions and the echoes reverberated to the summits of the Bavarian hills.

. . . And now back to reality. It is January, 1946 again. Nuremberg is desolate and strewn with wreckage. I visit the Stadium and stand in its vast emptiness. It is no longer alive and all the glory of its heyday is exposed in its tinseled cheapness. The monumental peristyle is a bleak concrete skeleton against the gray sky, the ground is mute and records no vibrating footsteps, the stands are

15

ugly with the moldy air of things which have forgotten, if they ever knew, human contact.

Nuremberg is dead. The city which had become the national shrine of the Nazi party today symbolizes the ruins of National Socialism and also, ironically, the destruction this explosive force wrought to the world itself. It was a wise decision on the part of the Allies to choose Nuremberg as the site of the war trials to determine the cause of the holocaust of World War II and those responsible for it. Thus, history would record that, as this city was the cradle of Nazism, it was its grave as well.

In a sense, Hitler parades again here in 1946, but this time with only a retinue of twenty-one persons. The parade route is a very short one. It extends from prison cells through a prison yard, into an elevator shaft and then into an indoor stadium not more than a hundred feet square. Here no bands wake echoes and no goose-stepping automatons pound the pavements. Each person in the procession is escorted by a helmeted, sturdy American soldier who leads him to a box in a brightly illuminated courtroom where he will explain the meaning of the roarings, growlings, and yelling in Nuremberg of ten years ago.

Hitler is in that courtroom, make no mistake of that. You may see him in the maniacal stare of Rudolf Hess, the booty-surfeited paunch of Herman Goering, the metallic chin of Hans Jodl, the stiff-necked stance of Field Marshal Keitel, the starched respectability of Hjlmar Schacht, the dream-shattered look of Ribbentrop, and the simian crouch of Reichsbank President Walter Funk. All together, with Kaltenbrunner, Rosenberg, Frank, Frick, Streicher, Doenitz, Raeder, Schirach, Sauckel, von Papen, Speer, von Neurath, Seyss-Inquart, and Fritzsche,

16

they make up Adolf Hitler who, through them, by them, and for them, brought civilization to the very edge of ultimate catastrophe, where it still agonizingly teeters. . . .

For nine months the Nazi high command listened to evidence of what they had done and which they never had thought would be regarded as crimes for which they would have to answer. On October 1, 1946, they heard the verdicts. Eleven were sentenced to death by hanging, three to life imprisonment, four to terms ranging from ten to twenty years. Three were acquitted.

Their trial was known as the International Military Tribunal trial (abbreviated I.M.T.). It was presided over by a judge and an alternate judge from each of the four allied nations. Great Britain was represented by Lord Justice Lawrence and Justice Birkett; the United States by Francis Biddle and Judge John J. Parker; France by M. Le Professeur Donnedieu de Vabres and M. Le Conseiler R. Falco; the Soviet Union by Major General I. T. Nitichenko and Lieutenant Colonel A. F. Volchkov.

Each allied nation had its own Chief Prosecution Counsel—the United States, Supreme Court Justice Robert H. Jackson; Great Britain, Sir Hartley Shawcross; France, M. Francois de Menthion; the Soviet Union, General R. A. Rudenko.

The indictment against the defendants consisted of four counts:

1. Conspiring to acquire totalitarian control over Germany, mobilizing the German economy for war, to construct a huge military machine for conquest and to commit war crimes and crimes against humanity.

2. Waging aggressive war against Poland, Great Britain, France, Denmark, Norway, Belgium, Netherlands, Lux-

17

embourg, Yugoslavia, Greece, the Soviet Union and the United States.

3. Violating laws and customs of war, specifying the murder and ill-treatment of millions of civilians in the German-occupied countries, deportation of other millions to slave labor, murder and ill-treatment of prisoners of war, killing of hostages, plunder and looting and unjustified devastation.

4. Crimes against humanity which included atrocities, murders, other offenses and persecution on racial or religious grounds.

Although the term "Crimes against Humanity" was one which came into being during the Nuremberg trials, the acts embraced in that terminology had long been recognized as crimes in civilized states. The principles governing these offenses had been assimilated as a part of international law at least since 1907. The Fourth Hague Convention provided that inhabitants and belligerents shall remain under the protection and the rule of "the principles of the law of nations, as they result from the usage established among civilized peoples, from the laws of humanity and the dictates of the public conscience."

It was under Count 4 that evidence was introduced to reveal to a shocked world the horrifying tidings of the slaughter of millions of Jews. Justice Robert H. Jackson, addressing the tribunal on this subject, said,

Adolf Eichman, the sinister figure who had charge of the extermination program, has estimated that the anti-Jewish activities resulted in the killing of six million Jews. Of these, four million were killed in extermination institutions, and two million were killed by *Einsatzgruppen*, mobile units of the Security Police and SD which pursued Jews in the ghettos and in their homes and slaughtered them by gas wagons, by mass shooting in anti-tank

18

ditches, and by every device which Nazi ingenuity could conceive. So thorough and uncompromising was this program that the Jews of Europe as a race no longer exist, thus fulfilling the diabolic "prophecy" of Adolf Hitler at the beginning of the war.

Although the law under which the Nazi defendants at Nuremberg were tried and many of them punished has now become an integral part of international law and has established a precedent which (at least morally) is binding on all civilized nations, the Nuremberg procedure has not had universal approbation. Admiral Karl Doenitz, who received and served a ten-year sentence as a result of the I.M.T. trial, has written his memoirs in which he says, "Whether any war is a war of aggression or not is a purely political question." He says also that there was no "moral foundation for the Nuremberg ruling, which condemned a soldier for an act that, at the time it was committed, was not a punishable offense."[*] August von Knieriem was another Nuremberg defendant accused of planning and waging wars of aggression and committing war crimes. He was acquitted and wrote a book in which he said that the fact a forbidden war is illegal "does not mean that waging it can be punished."[**]

Hugh Baille, former President of the United Press, says in his book *High Tension* that at Nuremberg the law was "extemporized for the purpose of hanging as many of them [Nazis] as possible."[***]

No less a public figure than Senator Robert H. Taft declared that our participation in the Nuremberg judgment constituted a "blot on the American record." He amplified: "I doubt if we can teach respect for principles of

[*] Admiral Doenitz, Memoirs (World, 1959).
[**] The Nuremberg Trials, von Knieriem (Regnery, 1959).
[***] High Tension, Harper, 1959.

19

justice by trying men for crimes which were not crimes when they were committed, contrary to all the principles of our law, which outlaws ex post facto condemnation." He added that it was a "novel and hypocritical procedure of the victors trying the vanquished for the crime of making war under the form of judicial procedure." When asked how he would have disposed of the men who with Hitler had caused death, sorrow and misery beyond all human reckoning, he replied that he would have banished them for life to an island in the middle of the ocean. But here his logic stumbled, for if the convicted defendants should not have been hanged because the acts they committed were not crimes, why should they have been punished at all?

In further explaining his position, Senator Taft said that the "making of aggressive war was not a crime when these men were the leaders of Germany." But if it was not a crime for the "leaders of Germany" to hurl aggressive troops into Poland, what was it? Is it legal for a nation to pounce upon a neighbor nation without provocation, excuse, or justification, and with but one object in view—plunder? Is it legal for a nation deliberately to repudiate a treaty in which it has said that it would not attack—and then, notwithstanding, attack? If the slaughterous invasion by Hitler of Poland was not a crime, the word has lost all meaning.

What is a crime? It is any act which the law condemns as injurious not only to the victim but to the general well-being of society and which makes the perpetrator liable to punishment. Within the boundaries of any individual nation the legislature and the courts enumerate and describe the acts which are prohibited as being criminal. However, in the relationship between nations, crimes are defined by custom, conventions, and treaties.

20

International law itself is accomplished by treaty and by the development of accepted practices. Thus piracy is conclusively acknowledged as a crime against all nations even though no specific and formal international document has so designated it. Thus also, a person charged with piracy may be tried in any nation where apprehended.

The same is true of slave trading. No international statute condemns it since there is no international parliament which enacts statutes. Nevertheless, slave trading is punishable in every civilized nation because international custom condemns it as criminal.

Aggressive war has from time immemorial been proscribed by the community of nations, even though, until the Nuremberg trials, there had been no international tribunal to enforce the proscription. When Hannibal continued to upset the peace of the Roman World with constant warfare, he was condemned to death by Rome in absentia, and eventually he committed suicide. When Napoleon repudiated the solemn pledge given in his Act of Abdication at Fontainebleau by quitting Elba, relanding on French shores, and rekindling the devastating wars which had plagued the continent of Europe, the Allied powers of Great Britain, Russia, Prussia and Austria, by convention signed at Paris, pronounced him an outlaw and banished him to St. Helena for life.

When Kaiser Wilhelm unleashed World War I, which drenched France, Belgium, and Russia with the blood of soldiers of sixteen nations, and reddened the seas with the blood of helpless passengers on countless torpedoed ships, the Allied nations decreed at Versailles that he be brought to trial for a "supreme offense against international morality and the sanctity of treaties." He escaped judgment because he had fled to Holland, which, as a neutral country, refused to deliver him up to the Allies. And there he lived out a long life amid every comfort and luxury that wealth could afford, relaxing in the woodland of his vast estate, undisturbed by the grief he had caused in millions of homes throughout the world. But, by that very provision in the Versailles treaty, Germany was made aware that aggressive war was illegal and so recognized by all nations. Germany formally acknowledged this fact on August 27, 1928, when she became the first nation to sign the Briand-Kellogg Treaty, later approved by sixty-three nations in all. The first two articles of that pact proclaimed:

I. The High Contracting Parties solemnly declare in the names of their respective peoples that they condemn recourse to war for the solution of international controversies and renounce it as an instrument of national policy in their relations to one another.

II. The High Contracting Parties agree that the settlement or solution of all disputes or conflicts of whatever nature or whatever origin they may be, which may arise among them, shall never be sought, except by pacific means.

In 1932 Secretary of State Henry L. Stimson said, "War between nations was renounced by the signatories of the Briand-Kellogg Treaty. This means that it has become illegal throughout practically the entire world. It is no longer to be the source and subject of rights. It is no longer to be the principle around which the duties, the conduct, and the rights of nations revolve. It is an illegal thing."

The famous English writer Rebecca West covered the I.M.T. trial for various magazines and later wrote out her experiences in a book. She paid her compliments to the critics who cried out that aggressive war was a "new crime." In vigorous language she retorted: "They spoke the very reverse of the truth. The condemnation of aggressive war as a crime was inherent in the Kellogg-Briand Pact."

Even prior to signing this Pact, Germany had acknowledged aggressive war to be crime. On September 24, 1927, all the delegations to the League of Nations declared that "a war of aggression can never serve as a means of settling international disputes and is, in consequence, an international crime."

World War II did not spring into being as the result of an uncontrollable outburst of wrath which, even as it drives human beings into excesses they later regret, sometimes forces nations into the excesses of mortal conflict. World War II was cold-bloodedly plotted, long thought out, and accurately planned with a meticulousness which would make poisonings by the Borgias, killings by Peter the Great, and assassinations by Catherine de Medici seem like acts of irresistible passion in comparison.

Many years before his tanks blazed across the Polish border, Hitler had announced in *Mein Kampf* that one day he would head a government which would expand Germany's frontiers. And then, once Fuehrer, he proceeded with his accomplices, many of them later defendants at Nuremberg, to draw treaties of friendship and nonaggression with the very nations he intended to attack, so as to lull them into a state of false security. Never was there betrayal of law and treachery to mankind on such a scale as was exhibited in this calculated violation of the pledged, written word.

Germany had entered into neutrality and nonaggression treaties with Poland, Austria, the Netherlands, Belgium, Czechoslovakia, Luxembourg, Norway, Denmark, Russia, and Yugoslavia. She invaded and made war on them all. In not one instance was Germany attacked first.

23

As a naval officer attached to the Fifth Army which fought its way from Salerno to the Brenner Pass, I saw many American helmets suspended from crosses over recently dug graves. After the armistice I saw similar American graves in Germany, France, Czechoslovakia, Yugoslavia and Austria. Why were these Americans here? And by whom were they slain?

Did not a duty devolve upon us to ascertain why they had lost their lives? And did we not have a responsibility to protect other Americans from the same fate? Or should we simply have let the dead past bury its dead and look to the future fatalistically? Germany had declared war on the United States. American ships had been sunk, American soldiers and sailors had been killed, countless American homes had been saddened, a crushing debt had been saddled upon the American people, our economy had been gravely thrown out of balance—and yet we were not even to inquire why? And were we not to determine if there was any criminal responsibility for this catastrophe which had been thrust upon us?

Did we not owe a duty to God and to humanity to ascertain the cause for this cataclysm? The most frightful war in the world had come to an end, twenty-two millions of people had been killed, beautiful cities were in ruins, what was once rich and luxuriant countryside now resembled the most forlorn wasteland. Europe was a vast cemetery, and there was scarcely a country in the world that did not wait for the return of bodies which but a year or two before were enthusiastic lads who had looked forward to a life of accomplishment, love, and happiness.

Untold millions of raggedy human beings foraged through ruins and rubble for an abandoned half-empty can of sardines or a discarded crust of bread. Society itself

24

had broken down. Human dignity staggered on the brink of extinction. The soul of man was in despair. Was this all to be ignored? Were those who were yet strong and still capable of thought to refuse the crying demand of humanity to bring order out of chaos and honesty out of the foul odors of lies, greed and cruelty?

World War II was not merely a war. It was a debacle of evil, a disaster planned and plotted by cunning brains and conniving hearts in an endeavor to subvert humanity itself. How could anyone rationally assume that responsibility for such a global catastrophe should not be legally adjudicated?

What was to be done with the coming of V Day? Were we to regard the late outpouring of blood as merely a sort of Olympics contest with winners and losers shaking hands all around?

Had we unlocked the secret of the atom, read the mystery of the stars, solved the riddle of the winds, and charted the bottom of the sea, only to stand tongue-tied and helpless before the task of holding man accountable for his crimes against peace, tranquillity, goodness and decency?

Were we to adopt the attitude that there always have been wars and there must be wars to the end?

But is it true that there must be wars? We have wiped out pestilences which from time to time decimated the earth's population, we have conquered malarial fevers, we have built barricades against floods. Can we not build intellectual barriers against man's greatest scourge? And if we are to make the attempt, must we not determine what and who causes war; and if criminal fault lies in starting aggressive war, should not criminal punishment follow, as it follows the perpetration of a single murder in times of peace? Because there was no hanging for

Frederick the Great, no shooting for Napoleon, and no garroting of Genghis Khan, all of whom, for power and glory, flooded continents with blood, must sanguinary aggression go on forever? Had the time not come to strip away the false honors won by mass killers and let them feel the shame, humiliation and punishment faced by the solitary peacetime murderer?

Was it not high time, in the calendar of humanity's struggle for recognition of the dignity of man and the universal desire for peace, to prosecute instigators of criminal wars?

Had the time not come to expose, with objective adjudication, the idiocy, not to say the criminality, of the statement made by Germany's idolized military hero, Field Marshal Count von Moltke, that "Perpetual peace is a dream, and it is not even a beautiful dream"? Von Moltke said further, "War is an element in the order of the world ordained by God. In it the noblest virtues of mankind are developed." Had the time not arrived to strike down such blasphemy?

Although the Nuremberg critics vigorously argue that there should have been no post-war trials, none goes so far as to say that the Nazi defendants should have been released with a whole skin. In fact, almost invariably they have maintained that, by all means, the "monsters" merited punishment. But how was this punishment to be applied? Rustem Vambery, Professor of Criminal Law and former dean of the law school at the University of Budapest, gave his idea: "There can be no difference of opinion about the necessity of exterminating the monsters who were responsible for the unspeakable horrors in Europe and Japan. That the Nazi and fascist leaders should be shot or hanged by the military or political power goes without saying, but this has nothing to do with law." But

26

how were the culprits to be identified except through the processes of law?

Nuremberg represents one of the noblest endeavors of all time to establish, on a permanent basis, order and responsibility between nation and nation and peoples and peoples. Never was there such a triumph for goodness, righteousness, decency and justice as was attained at the international war crimes trials. Here at last Evil was arraigned at the bar of justice.

Never had there been brought before a tribunal such a collection of refined cutthroats, intellectual assassins, world disturbers, and malignant egotists as appeared within the rail in the Palace of Justice at Nuremberg. Here it was demonstrated that the scales of justice may more evenly be balanced by law than by force.

Here was something to renew one's faith in the ideal of honorable relationship between man and man. That this supreme moral triumph brought criticism and scoffing from many who could not but have known better is disconcerting, but it cannot deter the steady progress toward fulfillment of the hope which abides in all mankind— truth and justice through law.

CHAPTER TWO

ONE OF THE SEVEREST CRITICISMS OF THE NUREMBERG TRIALS is wrapped in the thesis that military men were treated as criminals for merely doing their duty as soldiers. Even General Dwight Eisenhower was disturbed over the conviction of Field Marshal Wilhelm Keitel, Chief of Staff of the High Command of the Armed Forces; Colonel General Alfred Jodl, Chief of Operation Staff of the High Command; Erich Raeder, Commander-in-Chief of the Navy; and Karl Doenitz, successor to Raeder. He commented, "I was a little astonished that they found it easy to deal with a military man. I thought that the military would have provided a special problem." But none of the military was convicted because of honorable conduct on the field of battle.

The Army and Navy Journal, sharing General Eisenhower's preoccupation about the military, editorialized, "In our case, should we be defeated, the President, with his constitutional authority as Commander-in-Chief, would be hanged, and in company with him would be his personal staff and the chiefs of staff and naval operations, and were the associate justice [a reference to Jus-

28

tice Jackson] to have his will, the general staff, too, would be punished."

What a nation victorious over us would do, no one can prophesy, but there was nothing in the Nuremburg trials and judgments which would justify the execution of a nation's president or chief executive merely because he was the titular head of the country. It is to be recalled that the Emperor of Japan was not prosecuted. And then, it is to be noted, there were German generals who were tried but acquitted. In the "High Command Case," charges of conspiring to wage and of waging aggressive war were brought against Field Marshal von Leeb, who, next to von Rundstedt, was the most senior of all the German field marshals of World War II. With him as defendants were Field Marshal von Kuechler, who commanded an army in Russia under Leeb and succeeded him in 1942 as Army Group Commander, Field Marshal Sperrle of the Luftwaffe, five full generals, two lieutenant generals (who had held high field commands), Admiral Otto Schniewind (Chief of the Naval War Staff under Raeder), two lieutenant generals from Hitler's immediate military staff, and Lieutenant General Lehmann, the Judge Advocate General of the Wehrmacht. They were all found not guilty.

Adverse commentators on Nuremberg have said that German generals and admirals were tried for losing a war. This is not true. Colonel General Jodl was indicted by the Allied powers not because he lost a war, but because he was one of the coterie of conspirators who catapulted the world into a war of whose annihilating effects he could not profess ignorance. His diary matter-of-factly records the deeds of deceit, betrayal and treachery whereby the great crime of World War II was accomplished. It was Jodl who recommended that international

29

law could be circumvented by sinking an English ship as a reprisal and then expressing regret it was a mistake. Jodl was convicted and sentenced not as a soldier but as a conspirator against the peace and law of the world.

The same was true of Field Marshal Keitel, and Admirals Doenitz and Raeder.

Admiral Raeder was brought to trial not because he lost a war, but because with Hitler he repudiated solemn commitments in the Versailles Treaty and schemed with Hitler for the enslavement of nations which were illegally to be attacked, with the inevitable consequence of the shedding of much innocent blood.

Several days after he was sentenced to life imprisonment by the I.M.T., Raeder addressed a communication to the Allied Control Council asked to be shot. Acting under the directions of Admiral Glassford, I called on Raeder to ask why he made this unusual request. He said that he could not abide the thought of spending the rest of his days in a prison cell. I offered the consolation that there was always the eventual possibility of a parole. He said: "I'd rather die than live with a hope that cannot be realized." He repeated his request to be shot.

A week or so later, I went to see him to obtain information on some naval matters we had previously discussed, but I found an empty cell. A guard informed me that the Admiral had been taken to the hospital for a check-up of some kind. In a few minutes, however, Raeder returned, and I taunted him on his absence:

"You complained the last time I saw you about spending the rest of your life in this cell, but now I find you engaged in travel to heaven knows where."

He snorted. "Ach, they took me down there to the hospital to measure me for a truss because I have a hernia."

I expressed amazement. "Admiral, this is extraordinary. In the United States Navy we would never permit a truss. We operate. Surgery can cure a hernia quickly and permanently."

He answered, "That is true, Commander, but you know that you can die under an operation."

Raeder shammed as Hermann Goering had shammed. With much vainglory the corpulent field marshal had testified that he had supported Hitler's program because Hitler was establishing a new order which would benefit the entire world. A day or two after he left the witness stand I said to him, "Marshal, I do not understand your defense of Hitler. Hitler is the man who deprived you of your command and authority, stripped you of your decorations and ordered you shot. You only escaped death because we, the American forces, captured you before that sentence could be carried into effect."

He replied, "Commander, I supported Hitler when he was alive and I will support him in death."

I laughed in his face. "You know that you don't mean that."

He lowered his voice and looked around. "Commander, some day I'll tell you the truth."

He never got around to it. He took poison before the moment that the law arrived to escort him to the gallows for the expiation of his crimes.

The day after Goering's death, I called on Raeder and found him in a state of towering wrath. Because of the suicide, every object in the cells of those who had escaped the death penalty was being examined, studied, tested and analyzed as a possible depository for poison or other self-destroying agent. Every stitch of clothing was being scrutinized microscopically. Not knowing that the examination was in progress I arrived at the time when Raeder,

Doenitz and the other surviving defendants were without wearing apparel, and a sorrier group of would-be world rulers one could never imagine.

Raeder complained the loudest and most bitterly. He was sitting on the edge of his cot, the straw mattress of which had been removed, his bare knees shivering under a blanket wrapped around them. Over his naked shoulders he pressed tightly an unadorned navy jacket. "They wouldn't kill me with a bullet as I asked them," he grumbled between chattering teeth, "but they will kill me with pneumonia. What sort of treatment is this? Who is responsible for this barbarity?" And then, appealing to the code of gallantry in the profession of arms, he asked in high dudgeon, "Commander, tell me frankly now, is this the way to treat an enemy?"

The whole situation seemed a little comical to me, and I replied, "Well, Admiral, to tell the truth, it is hardly the way I would treat *a friend.*"

I requested the prison officer to give the shivering admiral his clothes, and soon he regained his suit, composure, and a fragment of his normal courtesy. Several hours later, however, I saw him in a state of despair which surpassed the emotion he had experienced in temporarily losing his attire.

Every afternoon the United States Army detachment on duty at the Nuremberg prison served hot coffee to the prisoners. On this particular afternoon Raeder was expounding some military theory when suddenly he stopped talking and cocked his ear to noises in the corridor. The music of the approaching coffee cart could be heard. "Commander," he said, "let's break off here. All day I wait for this moment of happiness and after what has happened today I need that coffee more than ever." And now this high officer who at one time could have commanded ocean-going tankers of coffee, thrust his nose through the bars of the cell, to await with tensed eagerness a tin cup of the steaming black fragrance which is the sailor's mainstay. As the coffee cart reached his cell he excitedly thrust forward his hand for the brimming cup, but his eagerness was too much for his nervous system, his hand quivered, he lost his grip, and the cup splashed to the floor, its contents flooding his feet.

"*Gott im Himmel!*" he cried with all the dismay of a captain seeing his ship torpedoed. "Sergeant! Sergeant!" he cried. "My coffee! My coffee!"

But the cart had already rumbled on, and the coffee man paid no heed to the wail of the woebegone mariner who turned to me, his eye dim with unshed tears. "Excuse me, Commander, for my emotional display. That coffee is the one thing which reassures me there is something worth living for. It is the only evidence there is some concern for us who have lost everything." He stooped over to retrieve the tragically empty GI container. I think he did this to conceal his mortification and to control his voice, which was breaking into a sob.

"Admiral," I broke in as rapidly as I could, because his outburst had left me momentarily speechless. "Don't worry, I'll see that you get your coffee."

"Will you?" he entreated, obviously with more ardor and sincerity than he had put into his plea to be shot.

In a few minutes the grieving seafarer was having his coveted cup, together with a couple of biscuits and butter. ·

"I shall never forget your intervention, Commander. I shall always appreciate this kindness," he gratefully moaned as he smacked his lips over the buttered biscuit and resuscitating drink.

It was this same sobbing fair weather sailor who had personally planned and carried into execution the criminal invasion of neutral Norway, bringing death and misery to countless innocent people. It was this same Hitler-accomplice who had said that he would abide by international law when it served his purpose but that when it prohibited measures favorable to his plans, those measures would have "to be carried out even if they are not covered by international law."

When Goering went on trial in Nuremberg, he complained to Dr. G. M. Gilbert, the prison psychologist who wrote *Nuremberg Diary*, "Bringing the heads of a sovereign state before a foreign court is a presumptuousness which is unique in history." But if violators of international law cannot be tried before an international court, there can be no assurance that they will ever be brought to justice. Under the terms of the Versailles Treaty, Germany was required to prosecute her own war criminals. The Allied governments prepared cases of prosecution against 896 Germans charged with war crimes. This list was reduced by the German government to a test list of but forty-five. Eventually only twelve persons faced a court and of these, only six were convicted, the sentences being for brief periods of imprisonment. Two defendants convicted of U-boat atrocities escaped, apparently with official connivance.

Had there been an international court (or what Goering termed a "foreign court") to try and administer suitable punishment to those responsible for World War I, the planners of World War II, knowing what would have faced them in the event they lost, might well have torn up their blueprints before tearing up a single treaty.

Albert Speer, one of the I.M.T. defendants, voiced this precise idea. As Reich Minister for Armaments and Munitions he was found guilty of war crimes and crimes against humanity, and was sentenced to twenty years' imprisonment. Shortly after he was sentenced I visited him at his cell and asked him how he felt about the penalty. He said that naturally he had hoped for an acquittal, but added, "I regret that your country, with Great Britain and France, did not try those responsible for World War I. If there had been such a prosecution, I would have been on notice what to expect if we lost World War II. I will admit we were warned; I knew that many of the things I did were not in accordance with the Geneva and Hague Conventions; but I never believed that you would do what you said you would do, and that is, bring us to trial."

Not the least of the achievements of the Nuremberg trials resides in the fact that they opened history's pages to the accused so that they could write their own story as to why their actions so convulsed society that seventy million men had to leave their normal pursuits to put on habiliments of war and take up weapons of death and destruction, and as to why such violence had to be done to the physical world that all the currency printed and the coins minted cannot make restitution for the lives lost and the property destroyed. That story of the defendants has now been written for all posterity to read —and it was written by the authors of the cosmic wreck which has had no equal since time began.

One day as I was leaving the courthouse I overheard a German visitor say to his neighbor, "I can't understand why the Americans are bothering with all this humbug. It is so childish. Why don't they just shoot these people?"

"Ja," replied the other. "But perhaps the Americans are thinking of history."

After the war General Lucius D. Clay, military governor of the American Zone in Germany, said, with the good sense and practical wisdom which marked his whole administration of military government in Germany, that the Nuremberg trials "were conducted in solemn dignity and with a high sense of justice." He said, "The mass of evidence, which exposed not only the relentless cruelty of the Nazi regime but also the grasping rapacity of its leaders, was convincing to the German people. They may have known something of the crimes committed by their own leaders, but they did not know the full extent of the mass extermination of helpless human lives, of the ruthless cruelty of the concentration camp. The trials completed the destruction of Nazism in Germany."[*]

The distinguished Walter Lippmann entertained an equally happy view of the Nuremberg procedure: "For my own part, I do not think it rash to prophesy that the principles of this [Nuremberg] trial will come to be regarded as ranking with the Magna Charta, the habeas corpus and the Bill of Rights as landmarks in the development of law."[**]

Still opposed to the Nuremberg judgments, some critics have said that the Nuremberg judges should have been selected from neutral countries. Justice Jackson commented on this subject: "Where in the world were neutrals to take up the task of investigation and judging? Does one suggest Spain? Sweden? Switzerland? True, these states as such were not engaged in the war, but powerful elements of their society and most leading individuals were reputed not to be impartial but to be either for or against the Nazi order. Only the naïve or those forgetful of conditions in 1945 would contend that he could have induced 'neutral' states to assume the duty of doing justice to the Nazis."

[*] Decision in Germany by General Lucius D. Clay, Doubleday, 1950.
[**] Ladies Home Journal, June, 1946.

36

As for having the Germans try the defendants, Justice Jackson trenchantly observed:

> To expect the Germans to bring these Germans to justice was out of the question. That was proved by the farcical experiment after World War I. But after World War II, organized society in Germany was in a state of collapse. There was no authoritative judicial system except remnants of the violently partisan judiciary set up by Hitler. And German law had been perverted to be a mere expression of the Nazi will.

Thus, anyone only half serious about the problem would have to conclude that if the Germans who were charged with ruining Germany and much of the world were to be prosecuted at all, the only countries which had the interest, concern, direction, and facilities to try them were the United States, Great Britain, France, and Russia.

And then, answering the criticism that the victors were trying the vanquished, it is enough to observe that in every community the judges are part of that element of society which enforces law and order and which causes the arrest and detention of those who appear at the bar of justice. To argue that because the judge belongs to that "victorious" segment of the state he cannot be impartial is to condemn the judicial system of the world. Under such a theory a German judge could not try a person arrested by the German police because the judge represents the power which, contesting with the defendant, was "victorious." Following such a doctrine, the army could not arrest and try deserters because it would be motivated by revenge in punishing the soldier who had attempted to do harm to the army. According to that philosophy of government, no nation could even prosecute tax evaders because it could be said it had a selfish reason to punish

37

the person who sought to withhold money from its coffers.

In every country the judges are paid by the dominant power which is the government, but this does not mean that they must be blind to the faults of the government and that they may not, therefore, render judgment against it and in favor of one accused by the government. It is by no means an infrequent thing for judges in democratic countries to decide cases against the government which pays them their salaries and invests them with authority.

Since Germany surrendered unconditionally to the Allies, the Allies could simply have tried the defendants as occupying powers and as the only government prepared to set up and run judicial machinery. But the Allies did not act on the authority inherent in victorious nations over surrendering nations. They pursued a course of action which guaranteed to the defendants all rights and privileges to which they would be entitled in a civil court under civilian control. In fact, the defendants were assured privileges which would not have been theirs even in a German court since the trial procedure finally agreed upon by the four powers included all of the advantages accruable to accused persons under Anglo-Saxon law and those assured him under the continental procedure coming down from Roman law.

Many of the Nuremberg faultfinders have been of the belief, or at least they convey the impression they are of the belief, that the idea to prosecute war criminals burgeoned into being only after the signing of the articles of surrender by Germany, and that, therefore, the defendants had had no warning that they might have to stand trial for what they had set out to do. Nothing could be further from the truth. The defendants were on notice before the first frontier was violated that there were standards of conduct under law which had to be met in conducting a war, even one illegally begun. Those standards on treatment to be accorded civilian populations were covered by the Hague Convention of 1907, and the Geneva Convention of 1929. That violations of the pertinent provisions in those Conventions constituted crimes for which the guilty individuals were punishable was universally accepted international law long before World War II began.

But awareness of what the defendants could expect for breaching international law was not limited to formal acquaintance with the Hague and Geneva Conventions, and general knowledge of the laws and customs of war. No document was so well studied and commented upon by Hitler and the reigning Nazi hierarchy as the Treaty of Versailles. In Article 228 of that treaty of 1919 the German government expressly recognized the right of the Allied powers "to bring before military tribunals persons accused of having committed acts in violation of the laws and customs of war."

Moreover, on October 21, 1941, Prime Minister Churchill, after President Roosevelt had condemned Nazi executions of hostages in France, declared that "the punishment of these crimes should now be counted among the major goals of the war."

On January 13, 1942, representatives of the nine Nazi-occupied countries (Belgium, Czechoslovakia, France, Greece, Luxembourg, the Netherlands, Norway, Poland, and Yugoslavia) proclaimed the St. James Declaration which placed "among their principal war claims the punishment, through the channel of organized justice, of those guilty of or responsible for these crimes, whether they have ordered them, perpetrated them or participated in them" and they resolved that the responsible persons were to be sought out and "handed over to justice and judged."

The Nuremberg defendants could understandably maintain that they never believed they would be brought to account for war crimes since, of course, they never thought they might lose the war, but they could not with any pretense at candor say that they did not know that in the event of capture they would have to face trials for deeds committed in opposition to proclaimed law.

On August 21, 1942, President Roosevelt declared, "When victory has been achieved, it is the purpose of the Government of the United States, as I know it is the purpose of each of the United Nations, to make appropriate use of the information and evidence in respect to these barbaric crimes of the invaders in Europe and in Asia. It seems only fair that they should have this warning that the time will come when they shall have to stand in courts of law . . . and answer for their acts."

On March 9, 1943, the Senate of the United States, with the House concurring, adopted a resolution which said, "The dictates of humanity and honorable conduct in war demand that this inexcusable slaughter and mistreatment shall cease and that it is the sense of this Congress that those guilty, directly or indirectly, of these criminal acts shall be held accountable and punished in a manner commensurate with the offenses for which they are responsible."

On October 20, 1943, a United Nations War Crimes Commission, made up of seventeen nations, began the gathering of evidence on war crimes and their perpetrators. On October 30, 1943, the United States, Great Britain, and Russia, in a joint proclamation issued at Moscow, declared that all persons taking part in atrocities and massacres would be prosecuted. The statement warned that "Most assuredly the three Allied Powers will pursue them to the uttermost ends of the earth and will deliver them to their accusers in order that justice may be done."

When the war ended, the Allies proceeded to make good their promises. In the summer of 1945 representatives of the four Allied powers met in London to formulate an "Agreement . . . for the Prosecution and Punishment of the Major War Criminals of the European Axis." The Agreement was signed by representatives of Great Britain, United States, France and Russia on August 8, 1945, and later approved by nineteen other nations. Thus, twenty-three nations empowered the International Military Tribunal to try the "major war criminals," that is, Goering, Ribbentop, et al. This Tribunal sat from November, 1945 to October, 1946.

The ending of the I.M.T. trial did not, however, terminate international criminal prosecution in Germany. The hundreds of tons of official documents captured by the Allied armies, the intensive questioning of prisoners of war by investigating teams, and the personal accounts of people who either had been victims of Nazi terrorism or had witnessed the killing and torturing of others piled up evidence of war crimes and crimes against humanity to such a height of horror that the Allied nations would have been remiss in discharging their international obligations, and derelict in moral responsibility, had they failed to prosecute.

No state or association of states worthy of the name of civilization could shut its eyes to concentration camps, gas chambers, inhuman medical experiments, genocide, and other brutal manifestations. If the vanquishment of Nazism was to mean anything in history, the individuals who administered those horrors had to answer to law.

41

Otherwise, the Allied winning of the war would be a mockery. Accordingly on December 20, 1945, the four Allied nations, speaking through their Zone Commanders in Occupied Germany, promulgated what became known as Control Council Law No. 10, which gave further effect to the Moscow Declaration of October 30, 1943, and the London Agreement of August 8, 1945.

This law enumerated four types of crimes: (a) Crimes against Peace; (b) War Crimes; (c) Crimes against Humanity; and (d) Membership in Criminal Organizations. Twelve trials were conducted under this law. General Lucius D. Clay, Military Governor of the American Zone in Germany, on recommendations by Alvin Rockwell, heading up the Legal Division of his administration, made the assignments of judges. John H. E. Fried, professor of international law, was Special Legal Consultant to the Tribunals.

I participated in three of the twelve trials. General Clay assigned me to the presidency of Tribunal II to try the third case, which became known as the Einsatzgruppen Trial. It is that trial which will be treated in these pages.

Although Control Council Law No. 10 seemed to have the outer characteristics of a statute, it was, in point of objective reality, a codification of existing international laws on the subjects it covered.

Perhaps no phrase was more often used by German defense lawyers at Nuremberg than the Latin maxim *Nullum crimen sine lege, nulla poena sine lege* (no crime without law, no punishment without law.) But is it true that there was no law which declared that the acts charged against the Nuremberg defendants were crimes when committed? Article 46 of the Hague Convention provides that "Family honor and rights, the lives of persons and private property, as well as religious convictions and practice must be respected." This provision imposed obligations on the German defendants not only because Germany signed the Hague Convention on Land Warfare, but because every country worthy of a flag has held itself bound to the rules or laws of war which come into being through common recognition and acknowledgment. Without exception these rules condemn the wanton killing of noncombatants.

The rules and customs covering war crimes and crimes against humanity have been the common heritage of civilized peoples for centuries. As far back as 1625, the celebrated authority on international law, Hugo Grotius, wrote:

> It is proper also to observe that Kings and those who are possessed of sovereign power have a right to exact punishment not only for injuries affecting immediately themselves or their own subjects, but for gross violations of the *law of nature* and of nations, done to other states *and subjects.*

The Nuremberg defense lawyers argued that the defendants were being prosecuted "under a murder law created ex post facto." But can there be an ex post facto *murder* law? An ex post facto law is one which declares to be criminal an act which when committed was not criminal. But was there ever a time when murder was not criminal? Professor Sheldon Glueck of Harvard University said of this argument of the German lawyers, "Even to state the German lawyers' proposition is to demonstrate its melange of impudence, cynicism, and absurdity."[*]

[*] The Nuremberg Trial and Aggressive War, Sheldon Glueck, Knopf, 1946.

The essential charge against the defendants in the Einsatzgruppen case was indeed murder. Whether any individual defendant was guilty of unlawful killing was a matter of factual determination but it cannot be said, with any historical sanity, that prior to the enactment of Control Council Law No. 10 there existed no law against murder. Law No. 10 merely supplied the tribunal for the trial of the crimes recognized since the dawn of creation.

> The great King of Kings
> Hath in the tables of his law commanded
> That thou shalt do no murder: and wilt thou then
> Spurn at his edict, and fulfil a man's?
> (Richard III, I, iv)

Military tribunals of the major nations have consistently tried and punished violators of the rules of warfare specified in the Hague Convention, even though the Convention is silent on the subject of courts. Prussia, in her various wars, and Germany itself, during World Wars I and II, employed military courts to prosecute subjects of other nations charged with breaching the rules and laws of war.

It is accepted legal procedure for belligerent nations to try individuals in their custody who are charged with transgression of international law. And if single nations may prosecute in such cases, with what more reason may a number of nations agree, in the interest of justice, to try alleged violations of the international code of war.

Counsel for the defendants in the Einsatzgruppen case, and in fact in all the Nuremberg trials, insisted that international law does not apply to individuals. But it is a fallacy of no small proportion to say that international obligations can apply only to the abstract legal entities called states. Nations cannot act except through human

44

beings, and when Germany signed, ratified and promulgated the Hague and Geneva Conventions, she bound each one of her subjects to their observance. Many German publications made frequent reference to these international pledges. As stated by Justice Jackson at the I.M.T. trial:

> The principle of individual responsibility for piracy and brigandage, which have long been recognized as crimes punishable under International Law, is old and well established . . . This principle of personal liability is a necessary as well as logical one if International Law is to render real help to the maintenance of peace.

Every German soldier had his attention called to restrictions imposed by International Law in his very paybook which carried on the first page what was known as "The Ten Commandments for Warfare of the German Soldier." Article 7 of these rules provided specifically that "The civilian populations should not be injured. The soldier is not allowed to loot or to destroy."

Article 4 of the Weimar Constitution provided that generally recognized rules of international law were to be regarded as an integral part of German Federal Law, and, as Sir Hartley Shawcross said in the International Military Tribunal trial, what could this mean, "save that the rules of international law are binding upon individuals?"

PART TWO

The Indictment

CHAPTER THREE

DURING THE LATTER PART OF THE WAR IN ITALY I WAS NAVAL
aide to General Mark W. Clark, commanding the American Fifth Army and then the Allied Fifteenth Army Group. After the termination of the war General Clark became American high commissioner of Austria and I accompanied him to Vienna where he appointed me President of the United States Board of Forcible Repatriation which passed on the Soviet Union's demands for forcible repatriation of Russian refugees.

Following this assignment of duty, Admiral William Glassford, commanding U.S. Naval Forces in Germany, appointed a Board of Review, consisting of Commanders Talbot, Reitzel and myself, to study the cases of Admirals Doenitz and Raeder, defendants before the I.M.T. in Nuremberg. After our report to the Navy on these two men, President Truman appointed me to the War Crimes Tribunal which was to try other defendants in Nuremberg.

I sat on the court which passed judgment on Field Marshal Erhard Milch, deputy to Goering, charged with war crimes and crimes against humanity. I was also a

48

member of the tribunal which adjudicated the crimes of Oswald Pohl and his accomplice-administrators of the concentration camps. Then, as already stated, General Clay designated me President Judge of Tribunal II to try the Einsatzgruppen case. My colleagues in this trial were Judge John J. Speight of Alabama and Judge Richard D. Nixon of North Carolina. Brigadier General Telford Taylor, succeeding United States Supreme Court Justice Robert H. Jackson as Chief of Counsel for War Crimes, appointed James H. McHaney as Deputy Chief Council. To prosecute the Einsatzgruppen case he assigned Attorney Benjamin B. Ferencz as Chief Prosecutor, who, in turn selected James E. Heath, John E. Glancey, Arnost Horlik-Hochwald, and Peter W. Walton as Associate Counsel. They were all able attorneys. General Taylor, a brilliant and remarkable lawyer and perhaps the most indefatigable and scholarly worker in law I have ever seen, participated in many phases of the actual trial.

There were twenty-four Einsatzgruppen defendants. (One committed suicide before the actual trial began). The indictment charged them with "the murder of more than one million persons, tortures, atrocities, and other inhumane acts."

Count One declared that the acts and conduct of the defendants constituted "violations of the law of nations, international conventions, general principles of criminal law as derived from the criminal law of all civilized nations, the internal penal laws of the countries in which such crimes were committed, and Article II of Control Council Law No. 10."

Count Two specified that the acts of the defendants violated international conventions, particularly Articles 43 and 46 of the Regulations of the Hague Convention No. IV, 1907, the Prisoner-of-War Convention (Geneva,

49

1929), the laws and customs of war, and, as indicated in Count I, the criminal law of all civilized nations and the pertinent provisions of Control Council Law No. 10.

Count Three charged the men with membership in the organizations adjudicated criminal by the IMT decision.

The word "einsatzgruppen" (plural of einsatzgruppe) may be translated literally into "deployed," "committed" or "replaced groups," but its most meaningful translation is "Action Groups." These Action Groups were semi-military organizations formed to follow in the wake of Hitler's armies to annihilate civilians proscribed by the Fuehrer. The most numerous victims of the fatal edicts were the Jews. In fact, as we will see later, other classes were added only to give a semblance of rationality to the charge that the Jews constituted a menace to the security of the Nazi state.

Since the principal part of the indictment, as indeed the evidence itself, was concerned with the defendants' slaughter of one million Jews, an explanation of the motivation behind these killings is in order.

It is now established biographical fact that Hitler manifested hostility towards Jews from his youth. As a young man he aspired to distinction as an artist. He painted postcards and drew designs for houses, none of which, however, brought him more than a few pfennigs of remuneration and recognition. In Vienna he flung himself into an art contest with a fierce determination to win first prize. The resulting prestige, he believed, would launch the brilliant career he had visualized for himself since boyhood. Furiously he sketched and passionately he plied brushes until finally he produced a painting which he thought must surely overwhelm the art jury with its daring conception and masterful execution. But the art jury rated it "a masterpiece of adolescent immaturity."

The enraged youth obtained the names of the jurors and concluded that four out of the seven were Jews. To the chairman he wrote a hot protest ending with the imprecation, "For this the Jews will pay!"

As Hitler grew older, he discovered many other things for which he felt the Jews should pay. He found that they were too successful—in business, finance, the theatre, the arts, the professions. But his severest charge was that they were responsible for Germany's losing World War I. Before countless gatherings he screamed, gesticulated and hysterically reiterated his accusation against the "international Jewish financiers who betrayed Germany into defeat," but he never spelled out just how or what the "international Jewish financiers" did which caused Germany to lose the war.

His idolatrous audiences, however, did not need evidence, logic, fact or reason. It was enough that a scapegoat could be found for the humiliation of Compiegne, the disgrace of Versailles and the hard times which had befallen the German people ever since the goosestep had ceased to resound over the cobblestones of the nation. After shouting themselves hoarse with approval and adulation his admirers surged into the streets crying, "*Nieder mit den Juden!*" And so, under the lashings of Hitler, now assisted by the fanatical whip cracking of Goering, Streicher and Goebbels, the Jews in Germany were ridiculed and despoiled, robbed and disfranchised, and thrown into prison and concentration camps.

But even these violences to person and spirit did not satisfy the demands of Hitler's hatred, which threatened to find added expression beyond German frontiers. On January 30, 1939, he shrieked in the Reichstag that if a new war came (knowing full well, of course, that it was on the way—he had already saddled the four horses of the Apocalypse), it would mean the "annihilation of the Jewish race in Europe." In September, 1937, Julius Streicher—appropriately termed by Justice Jackson the "venomous vulgarian"—had even surpassed Hitler. He shouted, "full and final victory will have been achieved only when the whole world is rid of Jews."

What might seem like macabre bombast was to become an unyielding steel-riveted plan of operation. Hitler did indeed set out to "rid" the whole world of Jews. The "ridding" was to be done methodically, efficiently and irrevocably. Hitler's chief in command of the operation would be Heinrich Himmler, the Reich leader of the SS organization and Chief of German Police. Next in command would be Reinhard Heydrich, chief of the Reich Main Security Office (referred to as the RSHA). The Reich Main Security Office, charged with maintaining the security of the Nazi state, was made up of seven units, handling respectively Personnel, Budget and Economy, SD Inside Germany, Gestapo, Kripo, SD Outside Germany, and Ideological Research. The fourth unit, designated Amt IV and devoted to the Gestapo, the dreaded German secret police, was headed by Gruppenfuehrer Heinrich Mueller. It was subdivided into six subsections, Section B being known as the Section for Jewish Affairs.

"Jewish Affairs" might suggest all matters appertaining to the Jews such as housing, food, clothing, education, religious worship, and so on. Since the Jews had become the principal target of the Nazis, one could believe that a special department had been set up to carry out specific types of confiscation, deprivation of civic rights, restricted ghettos, etc. This section, however—abbreviated to Amt IV, B4 of the RSHA, and housed in a building of its own—had but one function, and that was to work out the systematic annihilation of all Jews in

Germany and in all other countries which Hitler might subjugate. The man chosen to head this gigantic project was SS-Obersturmfuehrer Adolf Eichmann. He was peculiarly equipped for the satanic operation.

Rudolf Hoess, commandant of the Auschwitz Concentration Camp, who knew Eichmann intimately, said of him:

> Eichmann was absolutely convinced that if he could succeed in destroying the biological basis of Jewry in the East by complete extermination, then Jewry as a whole would never recover from the blow. The assimilated Jews of the West, including America, would, in his opinion, be in no position (and would have no desire) to make up this enormous loss of blood and there would therefore be no future generation worth mentioning.

When Dr. Brandt, one of Hitler's experimenting physicians, sought a collection of one hundred and fifty Jewish skeletons, it was to Eichmann that he turned to arrange for converting one hundred and fifty living human beings into the requested experimental material. He wrote: "By order of the Reichsfuehrer-SS, I therefore request you to make the organization of the planned skeleton collection possible." The request was fulfilled.

Adolf Eichmann was born in Solingen, Germany, in March, 1906, and early conceived an enmity toward Jews. So intense was this feeling that when he moved to Linz, Austria, as a boy, he mingled with Jews in order to learn their customs, traditions, and ambitions, anticipating that he could put this knowledge to use against them some day. He even learned some Yiddish and Hebrew expressions. Later he was to study the languages seriously. He sometimes organized teen-age gangs to beat up his own Jewish schoolmates.

After he joined the Nazi party and became an SS official, he invented the bizarre story that he was born of German parents in Palestine.

Three explanations have appeared for this story: (1) that Eichmann, himself accused of being a Jew because he associated with Jews and knew their language, invented the story in self-defense; (2) that his boast that he was a direct descendant of the teutonic Knights Templar of the Crusaders, who had fought in the Holy Land and remained there, was an attempt at self-glorification; and (3) that in posing as one who had once lived in Palestine he hoped that the Nazi hierarchy might consider assigning him there as an intelligence officer so that he could thereby obtain an even greater knowledge on all matters involving Judaism.

Whatever may have been the reason for the story, it seems to have been a factor in inducing his SS superiors to send Eichmann to Palestine in 1937. He landed there, with gold in his pockets, to bribe Arabs for information and assistance in his plans to organize a spy system in the Middle East. The plans miscarried because the British Government, holding the mandate for Palestine, ordered him to leave, but not before he had added considerably to his encyclopedia of knowledge on world Jewry. On his way back to Germany Eichmann stopped off in Cairo where he conferred with the Grand Mufti of Jerusalem on the latter's plans to harass the Jews in all lands subject to Arabic influence.

Because of this journey, supplemented by later trips to Jewish communities and settlements, plus an intensive study of all Jewish folklore, it was not long before Eichmann was being acknowledged in the Nazi hierarchy as the most learned and most experienced "expert on Jewish affairs."

54

Himmler placed him at the head of an establishment called the "Jewish Museum," which was charged with collecting and collating data on Jewish history, Zionism in all its aspects, the names, whereabouts and facilities of Zionist leaders in all parts of the world, and particularly the holdings of Jews, wherever located.

Eichmann so well displayed his talents in this field that it was inevitable he would come to the attention of Hitler himself, who approved of Himmler's selection and commendation of this unemotional but energetic architect of the Jews' eventual fate.

The mountain of Nazi records brought to the Nuremberg Palace of Justice contained countless charts, diagrams and sketches outlining the chain of command from Hitler down to the last corporal on the most distant fighting front. The chart of command from the Fuehrer down to Eichmann showed that all orders on "Jewish affairs" were to proceed from Hitler to Himmler, Himmler to Heydrich, Heydrich to Mueller, and Mueller to Eichmann. However, since "final solution" of the Jewish question was something very close to Hitler's heart, if one can use that term in so ghastly an association, Hitler sometimes wiped out the formal routes of communication and dealt directly with Eichmann in the project assigned to him for fulfillment. Certainly Himmler, who spoke for Hitler in all Jewish matters, ignored the intervening offices and conferred personally with Eichmann.

Thus Eichmann became the administrator of the most gigantic murder machine in the history of the human race. With his enthusiastically-acquired vast and detailed knowledge of all areas holding concentrated Jewish populations, he knew where the gas chambers and the cremation ovens could most advantageously be located; he knew the railroads and highways servicing these areas;

55

he knew how to conceal effectually the transportation of the victims to the murder mills.

Still he was not entirely satisfied with this method for the annihilation of Jews who lived in remote territories. First and foremost, there were the barriers of geography. He had already experienced difficulties in Europe in this connection. Transporting men, women and children in railroad trains and trucks required an extensive and complicated personnel of guards, engineers, firemen, interpreters, and so on. Moreover, railroad trains were needed to move troops; trucks were required to haul food, ammunition and all the impedimenta of war. Could not something be done to avoid the necessity of shipping Jews from faraway Lithuania, Esthonia, Romania, the Ukraine, and the Crimea to the concentration camps in Germany, Austria, and Poland?

Eichmann pondered the matter and finally arrived at what he regarded a very satisfactory solution. For such populations as could not be taken to the executioners, the executioners would go to the populations. Indeed it would be a waste of locomotive power and gasoline to transport peoples long distances just to kill them. In addition, there would be the expense and trouble of feeding them, sheltering them, and guarding them from escape before the mass executions. Eichmann reasoned, Why not kill them where they are found? How simple. No long waits, no costly maintenance of prison camps with barbed wire, guard towers, bloodhounds and electricity-charged fences.

Eichmann conferred with Himmler and Himmler conferred with Hitler. Eichmann's recommendations were accepted and the Einsatzgruppen organization was born. Thus, in the early part of 1941, Hitler directed Himmler, Heydrich and Eichmann to recruit mobile bands of executioners which were to accompany and follow the German armies as they smashed forward through Eastern territory, killing all Jews there as soon as any region or community was cleared of enemy opposition. Himmler removed all doubt as to the object of the Einsatzgruppen: "It is not our task to Germanize the East in the old sense, that is to teach the people there the German language and the German law, but to see to it that only people of purely Germanic blood live in the East."

The Einsatzgruppen organization was divided into four groups, lettered A to D. Einsatzgruppe A was to operate in Latvia, Lithuania and Esthonia, and Einsatzgruppe B in the direction of Moscow south of A's jurisdiction; Einsatzgruppe C would cover most of the Ukraine; and Einsatzgruppe D would do its work in the southern part of the Ukraine, the Crimea, and the whole of the Caucasus area. Each Einsatzgruppe was divided into Einsatzkommandos and Sonderkommandos, the Kommandos in turn being broken into smaller groups known as Teilkommandos. For the purpose of size and organization, an Einsatzgruppe could roughly be compared to an infantry battalion, an Einsatzkommando or Sonderkommando to an infantry company, and a Teilkommando to a platoon.

For men to lead the Einsatzgruppen Heydrich asked Eichmann for recommendations. Eichmann looked for men with exceptional ability and with a capacity for Semitic destruction as intense as his own. He found the ideal men for top leadership in Walter Stahlecker, Arthur Nebe, Otto Rasch and Otto Ohlendorf; and Heydrich appointed them, respectively, to head Einsatzgruppen A, B, C, and D. Rasch and Ohlendorf were eventually brought to trial. Stahlecker and Nebe were killed before the end of the war.

57

Eichmann laid out the course of action and from time to time visited the various units in the field to make certain that the scythe of extermination was sweeping as planned. While the Einsatzgruppen objective was plain enough, Eichmann camouflaged it to a certain extent. He asserted that the Jews constituted a menace to the political safety of all lands conquered by the German army, and thus were to be executed for security reasons.

He outlined the method of operation: As each Einsatz leader arrived in a city or any populous center, he was to summon to his headquarters the most prominent Jews in the territory (up to twenty-four, including rabbis), and inform them that, for the benefit of all Jews, plans had been made to resettle them in another area removed from the ravages of war. These prominent Jews would then be instructed to form themselves into a body to be known as the Jewish Council of Elders. This Council with suitable personnel would draw up a list of all the Jews in the area and direct them to assemble at a given point with all their possessions: money, deeds, jewelry, clothing, furniture—everything they could call their own. Solicitously, the couriers sent out by the Council would call at the homes of their relatives and friends to impart the good news of the resettlement, little knowing that the resettlement area was to be a lonely spot in the woods from which there would be no return.

Eichmann's scheme was effective. When the summoned Jews arrived at the rendezvous with all they possessed, their goods were confiscated in the name of the Reich. Then, with empty hands, the wondering travelers climbed into the trucks which drew up before them, and they were taken away to a previously designated execution ground, there to fall before firing squads. After this was done, the Council members, who were required to stand by to see how they had unknowingly been the agents for the destruction of their dearest ones, were themselves shot.

Occasionally doubts arose as to whether certain groups of individuals were to be classified as Jews or not. Evidence presented to us at Nuremberg disclosed, for instance, that when a certain unit of Einsatzgruppe D arrived in the Crimea, they found there a sect known as Krimchaks. No precise standard existed for determining whether the Krimchaks were or were not Jews and thus, if they were or were not to be shot. Very little was known of the Krimchaks except that they had migrated into the Crimea from a southern Mediterranean country, and it was known they spoke the Turkish language. It was rumored, however, that somewhere along the arterial line which ran back into the dim past some Jewish blood had entered the veins of these people. If this were so, should they be regarded as Jews and accordingly shot?

A radio inquiry flashed to Amt IV, B4. Eichmann assigned several clerks to look through encyclopedias and dusty books for information on Krimchaks. The clerks, knowing full well what answer they were looking for, since there was less chance of being reproved for resolving the question in the affirmative rather than in the negative, prepared a learned paper proving that the Krimchaks were Jews. From a wireless tower in Berlin crackled the message to the Einsatzgruppe forces in Crimea that Krimchaks were Jews and therefore were to be shot. They were shot.

Although Eichmann was certain that he would never have to answer to anybody for his deeds, there nevertheless apparently germinated in his mind the thought that the record might look less incriminating if the extermination program were not limited to Jews. No matter how far he had drifted from the anchorage of moral responsibility, he still knew that in the eyes of some people the slaughter of a people for racial reasons alone might be regarded as slightly illegal. The argument that Jews were a menace to national security had to be bolstered with some tangible evidence. Why not kill some other groups which could also be charged with hostility to the Nazi program for world betterment? Then it could not be said that the Jews were killed simply because they were Jews since many non-Jews would have been killed with them. Moreover, adding some other groups to the death list would in no way lesson the efficacy of the project to wipe out Jewry. Eichmann ordered that gypsies be added to the catalogue of the doomed.

Gypsies have rarely, if ever, been involved in the politics of a country in which they have taken up their ever-temporary abode. Since permanent residence was never their aim, permanent political domination could never be the purpose of their lives. Loving gay colors, they have down through the centuries brightened many a rural community with their colorful and picturesque garb. With an instinctive feeling for rhythm and tempo, they have enlivened country and town with a music all their own. Many of their melodious folk tunes were adapted by such celebrated composers as Franz Liszt and Johannes Brahms. Although they have sometimes baffled and annoyed with their incessant wanderings, indolent habits, occasional pilfering, and fantastic fortune-telling, no one had ever condemned them as a mortal threat or advocated their permanent removel from organized society. That is, no one but Eichmann and his homicidal hoodlum partners, with their maniacal plan to rebuild the human race in accordance with what they conceived to be the perfect, biologically Aryan civilization.

No Council of Elders was needed to select the gypsies from a cosmopolitan population. In their gaily painted wagons and tents they formed a bright patch on the landscape of any region and could easily be found. It was a simple matter to tell them they were to be moved, and it brought them no heartache to be informed they were to set out on another journey. Journeying was the very motif of their existence, traveling was the breath of their nostrils. They were told that for safekeeping they should place their violins, guitars, folded tents, extra clothing, gold bracelets, earrings and other jewlery into trucks which stood by. This done, they were invited to mount their wagons while some were loaded into other trucks. With smiles they obeyed and then, singing merrily, they rode to their new camping ground—an anti-tank ditch in the woods. There the smile faded from their faces and the notes of the song stuck in their throats as they beheld the guns in the hands of the Einsatz sharpshooters.

The Nazi blueprint, as evidenced by documents in Court, envisaged a purified race, and it was inevitable that weaklings, incurables, and mental patients would find no place in the Hitler temple of perfection. Therefore, the Aryan perfectionists asked themselves, why not wipe out all the unfits and misfits when the equipment for doing so was at hand? As the Einsatzgruppen forces rolled through vanquished lands, the flag of purity heading each column, it would be no trouble to empty the insane asylums, which, after all, occupied valuable building space which could be adapted to better purposes. Accordingly, the Fuehrer-Order, as the annihilating directive was now designated, was extended to kill off the mentally ill.

This extension often turned out to be quite convenient. On the outskirts of Poltava, a city in central Ukraine, one of the Sonkerkommandos came upon a farm operated by mental patients. The administrator of a German military officers' hospital within the city asked the Kommando leader to obtain at the farm a quantity of full cream milk for his patients. The leader investigated and found that the yield from the cows was only adequate to meet the needs of the mental patients, but the Kommando chief was equal to the occasion. If the supply could not meet the demand, he would diminish the demand. The chief reported: "A way out of this difficulty was found by deciding that the execution of 565 incurables should be carried out in the course of the next few days under the pretext that these patients were being removed to a better asylum in Charkow."

In southeastern Latvia a slight mistake was made and twenty healthy children, temporarily lodged in an asylum, were executed with forty mentally disabled children. The Kommando leader reported: "On 22 August 1941, mental patients from the Psychiatric Hospital in Daugavpils— approximately 700 adults and 60 children—were shot in the small town of Aglon. Among them were 20 healthy children who had been temporarily transferred to the building of the hospital from a Children's Home."

"Asiatic inferiors" was still another category destined for liquidation by the Einsatzgruppen. This designation allowed wide discretion. Einsatzgruppe and Einsatz- kommando leaders were authorized to take executive measures on their own responsibility. There was no one to dispute their identification of "Asiatic inferiors." And there was even less curb on homicidal operations in their authorization to shoot "asocial people, politically tainted persons, and racially and mentally inferior elements."

And so it was that in the spring of 1941, just as much of the world was wondering what possible further manifestations there could be of Hitler's proclaimed hatreds, Eichmann's Einsatz forces were gathering for instruction and training in the most ambitious hate-fulfilling expedition in the annals of time. The Border Police School Barracks in Pretzsch, Saxony, as well as the neighboring villages of Dueben and Schmiedeberg, became the assembly points for the expeditionary personnel which was recruited from SS and police organizations. The instruction and training of the enlisted personnel endured but four weeks and consisted almost entirely of rifle practice and listening to lectures and speeches on the necessity for exterminating the "sub-humans" who fell within the scope of the Fuehrer-Order.

Reinhardt Heydrich was the instructor. The Einsatz officers were selected from three notorious organizations, the very mention of whose names chilled the spines of all non-Nazis in Germany and German-occupied territory: the dreaded SS, the ominous Gestapo, and the sinister SD. The selected officers had all held important positions in offices or enterprises committed to the theory of the master race and, therefore, perfectly understood Heydrich when he spoke of liquidating asocials, inferiors, and subhumans. Several of them, when they became defendants in the Einsatzgruppen case, said that they had not comprehended the full scope of the Fuehrer-Order, but the evidence is conclusive that no other meaning was possible: the Fuehrer-Order called for the seizing and killing of Jews, gypsies, political commissars, "racial inferiors," "political undesirables," incurables and asocials.

The preparations for the Einsatz invasion were swift and the understanding complete. Only three days after Hitler's poised tanks broke into western Russia, dust rose from the roads leading out of Pretzsch, Deuben and Schmiedeberg as the Einsatz crusaders set forth, fully

63

equipped with rifles, pistols, sub-machine guns, riflemen, mechanics, interpreters, cooks—and gravediggers. Each vehicle carried the sign of the swastika, the symbol of the iron octopus, its tentacles reaching out to grapple and mangle whatever got between its savage jaws.

The Einsatz warriors needed no cavalry, cannon, or airplanes. There was no reconnoitering to be done, no surprise attack to fear, no enemy to combat. For them, the only resistance was that of distance; and besides, their cars, trucks and trailers were the very latest models in vehicular invention, and their drivers carried the newest road maps. But even if they did not reach any particular geographical objective at which they aimed, nothing was ever lost. There were always people to be found, and among the people in the vast reaches of land extending from the Oder to the Volga, and from the Baltic to the Black Sea, there were bound to be Jews, gypsies, lunatics, Asiatic inferiors, political commissars, Communist functionaries, and asocials—all helpless game for the resolute Einsatzgruppen.

The victories of the German armies turned out to be short-lived, but those of the Einsatzgruppen were permanent; they did not fly their flags over captured forts, capitols, and government buildings, but planted them in mounds of earth, over the silent multitudes who would never again populate the lands the armies had to leave behind.

PART THREE

The Modus Operandi

CHAPTER FOUR

THE STORY OF THE EINSATZGRUPPEN WAS NOT SOMETHING pieced together from memory years after their deeds had crimsoned the cities and countrysides of Europe; the story was written as the events occurred, and it was written by the doers of the deeds. It was written in the terse, exact language which military discipline requires; prepared with the cold factuality necessary to military forces in foreign territory; drafted with the care imperative in the planning of future operations.

The Einsatzgruppen forces had been instructed by Eichmann that each sub-Kommando leader was to inform his Kommando leader what his unit had accomplished each day, and the Kommando leader at the end of each day was to report to the Einsatzgruppe leader the total of the executions recorded by his sub-Kommandos. The Einsatzgruppe chief was then to transmit the records by wireless, mail, and (when occasion required) by courier to Eichmann in the Gestapo headquarters, Amt IV, B4 section of the RSHA. Finally, Eichmann would prepare duplicates of the reports and distribute them to Hitler, Himmler, Heydrich, Goebbels, Goering and the other

66

members of the Nazi hierarchy so that they might be kept abreast of the progress toward race purification which would assure the Nazi state a life of one thousand years, as prophesied by the Fuehrer.

With the fall of Berlin, the original Einsatzgruppen reports were found in Eichmann's headquarters. Benjamin Ferencz and a corps of translators studied them, and, with his assistants Walton, Glancey and Horlik-Hochwald, presented them to us in Court.

The reports, as they were read to the Tribunal, had but one subject. Only the actual language from some of these awesome records can convince a person that death could be treated with such cold-as-steel, businesslike matter-of-factness.

A chronicler for Einsatzgruppe B, marching through Byelorussia, could almost have been speaking of shooting rabbits or squirrels when he stated that on December 19, 1941, one of the organization's sub-units apprehended, on a road out of Mogilev, industrial and transportation center, "135 persons mostly Jews," of which 127 "were shot." It was not asserted that the Jews had attacked the Einsatz unit, or that they were enemies, or had demonstrated a hostile attitude, or that they had committed any crime. They were simply on the road, some on their way home to their families, some hurrying to their places of employment—most, certainly, minding their own affairs. But they were Jews, and they were shot. The same report announced with equal impassivity that a transient camp in the town "was searched for Jews and officials. 126 were found and shot." Then at a point near Bobruisk, a lumber center and clothing-manufacturing town, "a special action was executed, during which 1,013 Jews and Jewesses were shot." Not far away at Rudnja "835 Jews of both sexes were shot."

Members of Sonderkommando 4A, operating along the high banks of the Desna River in the Ukraine, like nimrods seeking wild ducks, reported from Chernigov that on October 23, 1941, 116 Jews were shot; and that on the following day 144 Jews were shot. A branch of this Kommando notified its parent unit that in Poltava, the site of the famous battle between the Swedes and the Russians in 1709, "altogether 1,538 Jews were shot."

Einsatzkommando 6, which stacked arms in the central Ukrainian city of Dnepropetrovsk, at the mouth of the Samara River, reported on October 13, 1941, that of the remaining thirty thousand Jews in the city "approximately ten thousand were shot."

From the seaport of Riga, capital of Latvia, Einsatzkommando 2, reporting as of November 30, 1941, sent tidings to Eichmann that "10,600 Jews were shot."

From Minsk, an industrial and cultural center with excellent medical and teachers colleges, the Einsatzkommando doing duty there reported in March, 1942, that "in the course of the greater action against Jews, 3,412 Jews were shot."

Einsatzgruppe D, reporting from a point near Simferopol, capital of Crimea, announced that "During the period covered by the report 2,010 people were shot."

An Einsatz unit tarrying for several days in the iron mining town of Rakhov, Ukraine, reported that "1,500 Jews were shot."

Hearing these reports in court, with their continuing drumfire of the word "shot," it appeared to listeners that the authors of the reports themselves began to tire of the staccato "shot," and thus attempted, within the narrow compass of expression allowed in military communications, to seek for variety in verbiage. One Einsatz commander, reporting from the capital of Latvia, related:

"The Higher SS and Police leader in Riga, SS-Ober-gruppenfuehrer Jeckeln, has meanwhile embarked on a shooting action (Erschiesungsaktion), and on Sunday, the 30 November 1941, about 4,000 Jews from the Riga ghetto and an evacuation transport from the Reitsch were disposed of." Until, however, Eichmann should become used to his versatility, this Einsatz writer felt he should define the new term he had used, so he added "killed" in parentheses.

Getting right to the point, a Kommando leader roaming through the peninsula of Crimea reported crisply, "In the Crimea 1,000 Jews and gypsies were executed." An Einsatz leader reporting on an action near a 17th century castle in the village of Lyakhovichi, Byelorussia, stated that "930 Jews were executed with the support of a Kommando of the SS Division 'Reich,' and then added with a proud flourish that "the village may now be described as 'free of Jews.'" An advance Kommando of Sonderkommando 4A, chronicling its activities in Pereyaslav-Khmelnitsky on the Tubezh River in the Ukraine, reported as of October 4, 1941, "Altogether, 537 Jews (men, women, and adolescents) were apprehended and liquidated."

Einsatzgruppe B, reporting out of its headquarters in Smolensk, Russia said of an operation in October, 1941, that "912 Jews were liquidated in Krupka and 822 in Sholopanitsche."

Other Kommando leaders used phrases such as "processed," "special treatment," and "taken care of." Not a few Einsatzgruppen chiefs recorded that certain areas "had been purged of Jews." Finally, there was one term which was gentle and polite, discreet and definitive. It in no way conjured up the heart-piercing picture of abject human creatures being shot and thrown into ditches. This piece of rhetoric proclaimed that in certain areas "the

69

Jewish question was solved." And when that wording was used one knew finally and completely that the Jews in that particular territory had been removed from the land of the living.

As report after report was presented in Court, each carrying its tragic tale, it seemed they were forming the successive waves of a red sea, its undulations crested with the black foam of misery and despair. From time to time a courtroom visitor would listen incredulously, stare unbelievingly, look at the defendants wonderingly, and then, quietly removing his headphones, steal out as if he had blundered into a museum of horrors.

The Einsatz leaders did not take their work lightly. Some of them cherished deep feelings. One report, which was introduced at the trial in the form of a letter, bared the bleeding heart of a Major Jacob of the Field Police, as he contemplated the task of killing Jews. Writing to his commanding general, the major sends birthday greetings, talks about his horses, his girl friend, and then about Jews: "I don't know if you, General, have also seen in Poland such horrible figures of Jews . . . Now of the 24,000 Jews living here in Kamenets Podolsk we have only a disappearing percentage left. The little Jews (Juedlein) living in the districts (Rayons) also belong to our customers. We surge ahead without pinges of conscience, and then . . . the waves close and the world is at peace."

He now chastises himself and imposes a severe self-discipline for the sake of his country: "I thank you for your reprimand. You are right. We men of the New Germany have to be hard with ourselves. Even if it means a longer separation from our family. Now is the time to clean up with the war criminals, once and forever, to create for our descendants a more beautiful and eternal Germany. We don't sleep here. Every week 3-4 actions, one time gypsies, the other time Jews, partisans and other rabble."

In another letter this officer becomes lachrymose and waxes nostalgic for his home and children. "One could weep sometimes. It is not good to be such a friend of children as I was." However, he does not explain what happened to the children who formerly lived in his present quarters. "I have a cozy apartment in a former children's asylum. One bedroom and a living-room with all the accessories."

One report submitted by the commander of Einsatzgruppe A complained that his organization had been delayed in taking up executions in White Ruthenia because of wearisome circumstances over which he had no control. And then, when these circumstances had been overcome, a further annoyance made its appearance: a heavy frost had set in, thus making "mass executions much more difficult." The commander was further nettled by the fact that the Jews "live widely scattered over the whole country. In view of the enormous distances, the bad condition of the roads, the shortages of vehicles and petrol, and the small forces of Security Police and SC, it needs the utmost effort in order to carry out shootings." One can almost detect in this report the wistful complaint that the Jews were quite unreasonable in not coming themselves over these long distances to present themselves for shooting.

One Kommando leader, learning that there were still 325 Jews left in the town of Nezhin, Ukraine, forty miles from Chernigov, lamented that he was unable to get to them for "special treatment" since "it was impossible to reach this place on roads which were covered with mud

71

after the rain and thus impassable for motor vehicles. Then there was a report which read: "Until now, it was very difficult to carry out executions because of weather conditions."

With regard to inclement weather, one usually associates it with something which spoils outdoor ceremonies, games, Easter attires and parades, as well as impedes travel and building operations. It is grotesque to think of it as affecting massacres which, in themselves, are calamities on so momentous a scale as to be beyond the influence of moisture—liquid or frozen. Still, all the logic resided on the side of Eichmann's executioners. Why should they run the risk of catching cold or even pneumonia? For what? To kill Jews who could be killed tomorrow or a month or two from now, just as well? Thus, the chief of Einsatzgruppe A believed himself quite logical when, in the winter of 1941-42, he sent the message: "The Commander in White Russia is instructed to liquidate the Jewish question as soon as possible, despite the difficult situation. However, a period of about 2 months is still required—according to the weather."

But it happened occasionally, that Einsatz groups fell so far behind in schedule that an acceleration in pace became imperative. One Kommando captain, manifesting annoyance at the fewness of Jews being killed in Grodno and Lida, in the lowlands near the Polish border, declared, "I gave orders that considerable intensification was to take place."

Whether it was an attempt to convince themselves that what they were doing was entirely justified, or whether they were engaging in euphemistic irony, one cannot know, but some of the Kommando leaders gave "reasons" for killing Jews. In Marina-Gorka, a little town on a railroad in White Ruthenia, the Jews were assigned to laboring tasks which, according to the Einsatz chief, were done

72

"very reluctantly." In order to expedite the completion of the task, the chief said that 996 Jews and Jewesses were given "special treatment."

One Einsatz commander, strolling through the streets of Mogilev, noted that in the vicinity of a cathedral some Jewish citizens were "extremely restive," and, in addition, were not wearing a prescribed badge. He was quite disturbed about this and called out a detachment of his men and shot twenty-eight of them.

In Minsk, a Kommando leader looking over a crowd of people, concluded that 733 of them were "absolutely inferior elements with a predominant mixture of Asiatic blood," and, therefore, according to Report No. 73, dated September 4, 1941, he had them shot. The report does not say what devices or standards he employed to determine the inferiority of character and the predominance of Asiatic blood.

In Radomyshl, a cotton milling machine town in the Ukraine on the Teterev River, there was, according to a report submitted by the Einsatzgruppe C chief, only a limited supply of food "for the Jews as well as for the children." Consequently, he said, "there was an ever-increasing danger of epidemics." To put an end to these conditions 1,107 Jewish adults were shot by the Kommando and 561 juveniles by the Ukrainian militia. Thereby, the Sonkerkommando has taken care of a total of 11,328 Jews till 6 September 1941."

In the ghetto of Newel, in the vicinity of Vitebsk, a city once ruled by Lithuania, then by Poland, and now by the Soviet Union, it was found, according to Operational Report No. 92, dated September 23, 1941, that the Jews were afflicted with scabies. The Einsatz commander moved in quickly. "In order to prevent further contagion, 640 Jews were liquidated and the houses burnt down."

The same report proclaimed further that close by, in

73

the town of Janowitschi, a contagious disease, accompanied by fever, broke out. It was feared that the disease might spread to the city and the rural population. To prevent this from happening, 1,025 Jews were shot. The report closed proudly with the statement: "This operation was carried out solely by a commander and 12 men."

As the Einsatz commanders became increasingly familiar with the therapeutic capabilities of the rifles in the hands of their men, they turned to the field of preventive medicine. Thus when a Kommando leader in the same city of Vitebsk saw that there was an "imminent danger of epidemics" he called out his men and shot three thousand Jews.

Einsatzgruppe C reported that a Teilkommando of Sonderkommando 4A, passing through Chernigov was asked by the director of the mental asylum in the city to liquidate 270 incurables. The Teilkommando commander obliged.

Operation Report No. 132, speaking of the activities of Einsatzkommando 5, between October 13 and October 19, 1941, said that in addition to executing twenty-one people guilty of sabotage and looting, and 1,847 Jews, it shot three hundred insane Jews, which achievement, according to the author, "represented a particularly heavy burden for the members of Einsatzkommando 5 who were in charge of this operation."

Report No. 150, dated January 2, 1942, referring to actions in the Western Crimea, stated, as if talking of cleaning out swamps, "Simferopol, Jewpatoria, Aluschta, Karasubasar, Keetsch and Feodosia and other districts of the Western Crimea have been cleaned of Jews."

Not infrequently, a report writer would embellish his written account with a sketch or map. Within the boundaries of the geographical area covered by his unit he

74

would draw a coffin and superimpose over it a numeral representing the number of Jews killed to that date. Outside the casket would appear another figure proclaiming the number yet to be killed.

Occasionally, an Einstaz chief would express rage over the unreasonableness of those he drove before him. One report told of Jews who, evicted from their homes, were obliged to seek primitive existence in caves and abandoned huts. The rigor of the elements, lack of food and proper clothing inevitably brought on serious illnesses. The Kommando leader communicated, "The danger of epidemics has thus increased considerably, so that, for that reason alone, a thorough clean-up of the respective places became necessary." And then he added, "The insolence of the Jews has not yet diminished even now."

Thus, after evicting, starving and shooting their victims the conquerors still complained that the Jews were not courteous!

The hand that struck the Jew usually managed to empty his pockets before he fell. Every live Jew paid for his heritage, not only with his life but with his home, land, and money—everything over which he exercised ownership. Every dead Jew gave up not only all this, but also his watch, fountain pen, jewelry, clothing and shoes. Eichmann even ordered that gold teeth and fillings were to be torn from the mouth of each victim after his murder. In some instances the dental gold was removed prior to the killings.

The prison warden in Minsk reported to the General Commissar for White Ruthenia, on May 31, 1943, that "On 13 April 1943 the former German dentist Ernst Israel Tischauer and his wife, Elisa Sara Tischauer, nee Rosenthal, were committed to the court prison by the Security

Service . . . Since that time all German and Russian Jews who were turned over to us, had their golden bridgework, crowns and fillings pulled or broken out. This happens always 1 to 2 hours before the respective action. Since 13 April 1943, 516 German and Russian Jews have been finished off . . . About 50% of the Jews had gold teeth, bridgework or fillings."

The pain and agony endured by one marked for slaughter between the moment that his teeth had been battered, his mouth lacerated, and his gums torn, and the moment he was to be led to his death, knowing full well what was to happen to him, curdles the ink of description.

No possessions were too extensive or too meager to be overlooked. Nothing was omitted from the gigantic program: everything from houses, factories and automobiles down to the last pair of baby shoes was stripped from the defenceless and unoffending Jew. Were it not for the accurate and full inventories prepared by the Nazis themselves, and the questioning scrutiny which a court trial affords, no one could believe that so vast a plan of thievery could be devised and carried into fulfillment.

Although no Nazi, alive or dead, has ever answered the question as to *why* the Jew had to die, there is no lack of evidence that the Jew's death enriched his captor, fattened his oppressor, and filled the bloodstained pocket of his assassin. The Nazi leaders and their followers detested, hated, and loathed the Jews, but nonetheless they carried their watches, wrote with their fountain pens, wore their clothing and masticated with the gold taken from the teeth of those they slew.

It would appear that occasionally raids were made in order to obtain specific garments. The defendant SS-Major Waldemar Klingelhoefer related how he was ordered by his Einsatzgruppe leader "to go from Smolensk to Tatarsk and Mstislavl to get furs for the German troops and to liquidate part of the Jews there." When he was asked whether the men rounded up in this raid were undressed before the execution he replied: "No, the clothing wasn't taken—this was a fur coat procurement operation."

A document originating in Einsatzgruppe D headquarters (February 1942) spoke of the "confiscation" of watches in the course of executions. Some of the gold and silver timepieces were sent to Berlin, others were handed over to the Wehrmacht (rank and file) and the remainder to members of the Einsatzgruppe itself "for a nominal price" or even gratuitously if the circumstances warranted that kind of liberality. The report also stated that part of the money seized was required for "routine purposes (wages etc.)." Thus the executioners paid themselves with money taken from the persons they had robbed and killed. The Einsatzgruppe recorded, in addition, that it helped Ethnic German families living in southern Russia by placing Jewish homes, furniture, children's beds, and other equipment at their disposal.

Einsatzgruppe C, boldly announcing its accomplishments in Korowo (September 1941), pointed out how it had organized a regular police force to clear the country of Jews as well as for other purposes. The men enlisted for all these purposes, the report went on to say, received "their pay from the municipality from funds seized from Jews."

This same organization, reporting on October 7, 1941, assured Amt IV, B4 that the crowded housing conditions in Kiev had been somewhat ameliorated because "an adequate number of apartments had been evacuated through the liquidation of approximately 35,000 Jews."

The Jewish Councils of Elders, when appointed, were

77

ordered by the Einsatz leaders to supply detailed data on all possessions of the Jews so that the despoilers would not have to lose time in harvesting the fruits of their quests before moving into other orchards. With these lists, the Einsatz chieftains could gather in, as if with a rake, all the Jews' property without even having to look for it.

The evidence produced at the trial unfolded a vast blood-framed backdrop for the endless executions. Nearly always an attempt was made to line up the human targets in a deep wood with only trees and incredulous beasts of the forest as witnesses. Sometimes ranges of mountains picked up the echoes of the rifle fire which decimated the population they had sheltered. Other times the killings occurred by the shores of a river, lake or creek reddened by the extravasated blood. Often, the ruins of a burned-out village provided the stage for the cruel drama, inconceivable outside the brain of an insane playwright and a mad producer.

What, indeed, no dramatist would ever invent, the Einsatzgruppen leaders planned and executed, and they kept records of what they did. Thus one is not called upon to speculate how one million killings were accomplished. One is not compelled to guess as to the modus operandi. On this subject, as indeed on all subjects involving the Nazi regime, the baleful plot is well documented. The deeds of the Nazis were dark but their perpetrators never failed to supply torches, by way of written records, oral statements, and frank demonstration, to light up what they wrote in the book of evil.

The reports also disclosed that most Kommando leaders were very considerate of their riflemen. Some of them would allow a pause between volleys so that the more fastidious of the executioners could light up cigarettes. As the gunsmoke settled, they puffed tranquilly, the scent of the tobacco mingling with the sweet offensiveness of the spilled blood.

There were squad men who did not like the task of cleaning up the ground when the bodies did not fall directly into the grave. Accordingly, a method was devised to avoid this supplementary exertion. The prisoners were led into the grave while still alive. One SS eyewitness explained, "The people were executed by a shot in the neck. The corpses were buried in a large tank ditch. The candidates for execution were already standing or kneeling in the ditch. One group had scarcely been shot before the next came and laid themselves on the corpses there."

Executions were always efficiency-perfect performances, illustrated by Report No. 24, dated July 16, 1941, which succinctly recorded, "The arrested Jewish men are shot without ceremony and interred in already prepared graves, the ED 1B having shot 1,150 Jews at Duenburg up to now."

Some of the Kommando leaders, however, perhaps more concerned about the eternal fitness of things, felt that a little ceremony was required. Accordingly they called off the names of the doomed persons before they were loaded on to the truck. This was the whole judicial trial—the indictment, the evidence, and the sentence—a roll call of death.

The usual rule that executions were not to be performed publicly was occasionally not adhered to. One report described an execution which took place near houses whose occupants became unwilling witnesses to the macabre scene:

"A heavy supply traffic for the soldiers was also going on in the main street, as well as traffic of evacuated civil-

79

ians. All events could be followed from the window of the battalion's office, the moaning of the people to be shot could be heard, too. The following morning, a lot of clothing was lying about the place concerned [and] surrounded by inquisitive civilians and soldiers."

Not only did the Einsatzgruppen carry out their own killings, but where they invaded communities already predisposed against Jews, they whipped up passions which often exploded into massacres known as pogroms.

Hermann Friedrich Graebe, manager and engineer in charge of a German building firm in Sdolbunow, Ukraine, narrated in graphic language how a pogrom operates. When he heard that one of these horrifying performances was being rehearsed in his town he called on the commanding officer of the area, SS-Sturmbannfuehrer Puetz, to make inquiries, since he, Graebe, employed a few Jewish workers he wished to protect. Sturmbann-fuehrer Puetz denied the rumors. Later, however, Graebe ascertained from the Area Commissioner's deputy, Stabs-leiter Beck, that what he heard was true, but Beck exacted from Graebe the promise not to disclose the secret. In exchange for this promise, he supplied Graebe with a certificate which was to protect his workers when the storm of blood should burst. This amazing document reads:

"Messrs. JUNG
R O V N O
The Jewish workers employed by your firm are not affected by the pogrom (Aktion). You must transfer them to their new place of work by Wednesday, 15 July 1942, at the latest.

From the Area Commissioner Beck"

That evening the pogrom lashed through the streets of

80

Rovno like a hurricane. Let Graebe tell the story in his own words:

> The people living there were driven on to the street just as they were, regardless of whether they were dressed or in bed. Since the Jews in most cases refused to leave their houses and resisted, the SS and militia applied force. They finally succeeded, with strokes of the whip, kicks and blows, with rifle butts in clearing the houses. The people were driven out of their houses in such haste that small children in bed had been left behind in several instances. In the street women cried out for their children and children for their parents. That did not prevent the SS from driving the people along the road, at running pace, and hitting them, until they reached a waiting freight train.
>
> Car after car was filled, and the screaming of women and children, and the cracking of whips and rifle shots resounded unceasingly. Since several families or groups had barricaded themselves in especially strong buildings, and the doors could not be forced with crowbars or beams, these houses were now blown open with hand grenades. Since the Ghetto was near the railroad tracks in Rovno, the younger people tried to get across the tracks and over a small river to get away from the Ghetto area. As this stretch of country was beyond the range of the electric lights, it was illuminated by signal rockets.
>
> All through the night these beaten, hounded and wounded people moved along the lighted streets. Women carried their dead children in their arms, children pulled and dragged their dead parents by their arms and legs down the road toward the train. Again and again the cries "Open the door! Open the door!" echoed through the Ghetto.

Despite the immunity guaranteed Graebe's Jewish workers by Commissioner Beck, seven of them were

81

seized and taken to the collecting point. Graebe's narrative continues:

I went to the collecting point to save these seven men. I saw dozens of corpses of all ages and both sexes in the streets I had to walk along. The doors of the houses stood open, windows were smashed. Pieces of clothing, shoes, stockings, jackets, caps, hats, coats, etc. were lying in the street. At the corner of the house lay a baby, less than a year old with his skull crushed. Blood and brains were spattered over the house wall and covered the area immediately around the child. The child was dressed only in a little shirt.

The commander, SS Major Puetz, was walking up and down a row of about 80-100 male Jews who were crouching on the ground. He had a heavy dog whip in his hand. I walked up to him, showed him the written permit of Stabsleiter Beck and demanded the seven men whom I recognized among those who were crouching on the ground. Dr. Puetz was very furious about Beck's concession and nothing could persuade him to release the seven men. He made a motion with his hand encircling the square and said that anyone who was once here would not get away. Although he was very angry with Beck, he ordered me to take the people from 5 Bahnhofstrasse out of Rovno by 8 o'clock at the latest.

When I left Dr. Puetz, I noticed a Ukrainian farm cart, with two horses. Dead people with stiff limbs were lying on the cart, legs and arms projected over the side boards. The cart was making for the freight train. I took the remaining 74 Jews who had been locked in the house to Sdolbunow.

Five thousand Jews were killed in this pogrom.

Often at Nuremberg a sadness akin to hopeless resignation inundated my soul. How could I accept the concept of a planned and calculated destruction of a race of human beings? It was so completely fantastic and devoid of sense that one wished not to hear any more about it and at times hoped he could turn a deaf ear to what seemed arrant nonsense. Barbarous tribes in the wilds of impenetrable jungles have fallen upon other tribes and destroyed their every member; ancient and medieval despots decreed the extermination of life in cities and regions; in Wild West days Indian uprisings wiped out caravans and destroyed whole settlements; but that an enlightened people in the twentieth century should set out to completely eradicate another enlightened people, not in battle, not by frenzied mobbing, but by calculated shooting, gassing, and burning, seemed like blood-curdling fiction, fit companion for H. G. Wells' chimera of the invasion from Mars.

Were it not that the officially authenticated reports and the testimony of the defendants themselves, plus eye-witnesses, verified the happening of these events, they would have to be dismissed as alcoholic or opium-dreaming invention. Even before the trial, Allied investigators and analysts checked and rechecked the Einsatz documentation. Being human, they sometimes doubted the correctness of the startling murder figures appearing in the reports.

SS-General Stahlecker, heading Einsatzgruppe A, did not live to stand trial for his crimes but he left carefully kept statistics which disclosed that in four months his unit killed 135,000 Jews. General Otto Ohlendorf, who will later be considered at length, had been questioned on the authenticity of this report since the number, in view of the brief period involved, seemed rather high. Ohlendorf studied the document almost indulgently, as if to ask: "Why should people be so incredulous?" and then said, "I have seen the report of Stahlecker (Document L-180) concerning Einsatzgruppe A, in which Stahlecker asserts that his group killed 135,000 Jews and Communists in the first four months of the program. I know Stahlecker personally, and I am of the opinion that the document is authentic."

How can all this be explained? Even when Germany was retreating on all fronts, troops which were desperately needed to stem the Allied drive were diverted to support this insane mission of extermination. In defiance of military needs, in spite of economic demands, and against every rule of reason, incalculable manpower was being wildly killed off and irreplaceable property was being destroyed.

Here and there a protest was raised. The SS-Commissioner General for White Ruthenia objected to the executions in his territory—not, to be sure, on the grounds of humanity, but because he believed the unbridled murder program struck at Germany's prestige. "Above all, any act lowering the prestige of the German Reich and its organizations in the eyes of the White Ruthenian population should be avoided . . . I am submitting this report in duplicate so that one copy may be forwarded to the Reich Minister. Peace and order cannot be maintained in White Ruthenia with methods of that sort. To bury seriously wounded people alive who worked their way out of their graves again, is such a base and filthy act that this incident as such should be reported to the Fuehrer and Reich Marshal."

For a country at war nothing can be more vital than that ammunition reach the soldiers holding the fighting fronts. Yet, in a massacre in Sluzk, vehicles loaded with ammunition for the armed forces were left standing in the streets because the Jewish drivers, already illegally forced into this service, had been liquidated by the

Execution Battalions. Although the very life of the nation depended on the continued operation of every type of food-producing establishment, fifteen of the twenty-six specialists at a cannery were shot.

This blood bath of Sluzk brought about some interesting correspondence. The Commissioner General inquired of the Reich Minister of the Occupied Eastern Territories if the liquidation of Jews in the East was to take place without regard to the economic interests of the Wehrmacht and specialists in the armament industry. The Reich Minister replied, "Clarification of the Jewish question has most likely been achieved by now through verbal discussions. Economic considerations should fundamentally remain unconsidered in the settlement of the problem."

Occasionally, families were spared because the breadwinners produced articles needed for the German army. The sparing, however, was strictly temporary. Einsatzgruppe C, reporting on conditions in Nowo-Ukrainia, stated that the only good harnessmakers and tailors were Jews. Also that in other places "only Jews can be employed for carpentry and locksmith work." Therefore, "in order not to endanger reconstruction and the repair work also for the benefit of transient troop units, it has become necessary to exclude provisionally especially the older Jewish skilled workers from the executions."

Eichmann, however, was opposed to this provisional exclusion of Jews from the execution program because, he said, this offered a chance for the Jews to contrive an escape, and this would delay accomplishment of the "complete destruction of biological Jewry."

He was supported in this position by Heinrich Himmler. In September, 1941, Himmler and Eichmann visited General Otto Ohlendorf, commanding Einsatzgruppe D, operating at the time out of Nikolayev in the south

Ukrainian lowlands. Ohlendorf had ordered a few days' postponement in the shooting of Jewish farm workers so that they could bring in the harvest for shipment back to Germany, the bulk of whose farmers were in the army. Even though Ohlendorf was a personal friend of Eichmann's, both he and Himmler upbraided Ohlendorf, the postponement order was cancelled and the Jewish farmers perished with the unharvested crops in the fields.

A German inspector of armament in the Ukraine, after a thorough investigation into the Jewish liquidation program, reported to General of the Infantry Thomas, Chief of the Industrial Armament Department, that the project was a big mistake from the German point of view. In the Ukraine he found that the Jews represented almost the entire trade and even a substantial part of the manpower. "The elimination, therefore, necessarily had far-reaching economic consequences and even direct consequences for the armament industry (Production for supplying the troops)."

In a final appeal to reason this German inspector cried out, "If we shoot the Jews, let the prisoners of war perish, condemn considerable parts of the urban population to death by starvation and also lose a part of the farming population by hunger during the next year, the question remains unanswered: Who in all the world is then supposed to produce economic values here?"

No one answered the question of the German inspector. Nor did anyone answer the question of Humanity as to the reason for this deluge of blood. Reason, with its partner Conscience, had been lost long ago in the jungle of Nazi greed and arrogance, and so Madness ruled, Hate marched, the sky reddened with the flames of destruction and the world wept—and still weeps.

PART FOUR

The Trial

CHAPTER FIVE

OLD NUREMBERG HAD A STORYBOOK CHARM WITH ITS ancestral castles, ancient towers, baroque steeples and medieval walls, and it was famed for its impressive contributions to German culture.

It was in Nuremberg that the Meistersingers once chanted their "rude poetic strains," many of which Richard Wagner set to music. It was here that bells of medieval melodiousness called the peaceful burghers to church, to concert, and to rest. And it was here that the standard of living was of the highest. In Nuremberg, artists, poets and composers flourished, and here happy townfolk fashioned toys which entranced a blithe and credulous world.

But in September, 1935, Adolf Hitler brought a toy of his own to Nuremberg, a Frankenstein contrivance which he controlled with greater ease than any little girl could handle a speaking doll. The toy was his personally chosen Reichstag. Responding quickly to its master's touch, this puppet belched forth the Hitlerian edicts which drove the Jews of Germany into ghettos, expelled them from the professions, expropriated their property, prohibited them the use of educational and cultural facilities, stripped them of German citizenship, and compelled them to wear distinctive, humiliating insignia. These edicts became known as the Nuremberg laws. For the following ten years, the name of Nuremberg evoked in the consciousness of the world the ever-continuing vision of Nazi iron-heeled boots trampling over helpless victims. After the Allied Normandy landing, Nuremberg was resolved into a military fortress and garrisoned with veteran SS troops who were pledged not to yield this emblem of Nazi supremacy, no matter what the cost in life.

On January 2, 1945, the Nuremberg decrees of 1935 perished. An Allied air armada cancelled out the Frankenstein statutes, but in the annihilating process the city's medieval walls fell, the towers crashed, the steeples toppled and the moats filled with the wreckage of what was once the most entrancing city of all Deutschland. Paradoxically, in all the hell's confetti which fell upon Nuremberg as if in some satanic mardi gras, the two mammoth structures which more than any others symbolized the target of the fiery attack, escaped destruction. One was the vast stadium in which Germany's strident voice had harangued the multitudes into hysteria; the other was the Palace of Justice in which the victims of that hysteria drank the bitter dregs of injustice. Although several bombs landed on the Palace, one of its wings collapsed, windows disintegrated, floors sagged and machine gun bullets chipped at the massive pillars upholding the façade, the building still reared a proud and unbowed head.

On April 20th, Hitler's birthday, American troops, under the protection of a thunderous artillery barrage, slipped through the smoking ruins and captured the city, and the Stars and Stripes displaced the swastika on its stony summit. An antiaircraft company, taking over the Palace, converted the judicial bench into a bar, introducing kegs of beer into the austere judges' chambers. The Palace, which had been erected before the Nazis seized power, seemed to know, however, that before long it would regain its original dignity as a mansion dedicated to law—no matter how often, in recent years, that law had been perverted within its ornate walls.

The war over, the victorious Allies proceeded, as they had said they would, to indict those responsible for it. For historical emphasis, Nuremberg was the ideal locale for the trial. Immediately, an army of workmen moved on the Palace of Justice. With the alacrity of bees repairing a hive after an invasion of bears, they bricked up the bomb holes, hurried away the debris and wreckage, tore out the old bench-bar, and rolled away the beer kegs. Architects, masons, carpenters, plasterers, and electricians swarmed through the citadel and soon the main courtroom became a triumph of modern craftsmanship. Heavy carpets now covered the stone floors—and they were to know footsteps that once shook the world. Generals, admirals, statesmen, administrators, diplomats, scientists, historians and soldiers from all parts of the globe would be making up part of each day's great population of defendants, prosecutors, jurists, witnesses, consultants, and observers in this erstwhile Nazi stronghold. One stood here at the Bar of History itself.

The judges' bench along the west wall stretched about two-thirds the length of the room; the defendants' dock against the east wall faced the judges and consisted of two long wooden benches with space to accommodate up to twenty-four persons. A glass enclosure in a corner to the left of the dock housed a corps of interpreters, specially trained to integrate their translations so that an

90

auditor could listen in any one of four languages by simply setting the switch on the chair arm to English, French, German or Russian. Since all speaking was done into a microphone, no one raised his voice and, as a consequence, anyone stepping into the large courtroom, and not wearing earphones, encountered a curious effect of dead silence. Such a visitor, seeing the lawyers stand up, extend their arms and move their lips—yet hearing no words, and watching witnesses reply with soundless voices—could not fail to get the sensation of watching a motion picture with the sound track shut off.

Other parts of the building were also rebuilt and renovated for use as offices, photo laboratories, document depositories, guard rooms, and additional courtrooms.

Much of the Einsatzgruppen trial unfolded in what was known as Courtroom No. 2, but frequently we sat in the main courtroom where, on September 29, 1947, Benjamin Ferencz, chief prosecutor, made the opening speech for the prosecution.

Because Mr. Ferencz was short of stature, his head barely cleared the lectern, but what he said in that impressive setting made him seem like a Thor striking with a mighty hammer as he told of the slaughterous deeds of the Einsatzgruppen leaders.

Since the twenty-three defendants were charged with one million murders, one would expect to see in the dock a band of coarse, untutored barbarians. Instead, one beheld a group of men with a formidable educational background. Looking at them from left to right we saw:

First Row:

SS-Major General Otto Ohlendorf, Chief of Einsatzgruppe D. Graduated in law and political science from the Universities of Leipzig and Goettingen. A one-time practicing barrister in the courts of Alfeld-Leine and Hildesheim.

SS-Brigadier General Heinz Jost, Chief of Einsatzgruppe A. Specialized in law and economics when he studied at the Universities of Giessen and Munich.

SS-Brigadier General Erich Naumann, Chief of Einsatzgruppe B. Left school at age of 16 and entered commercial firm. Later became officer of police.

SS-Brigadier General Otto Rasch. Doctor of Law and Economics, former mayor of Wittenberg.

SS-Brigadier General Erwin Schulz. Studied law at University of Berlin and later became staff member of Dresden Bank.

SS-Brigadier General Franz Six. Full time university professor.

SS-Colonel Paul Blobel. Former architect.

SS-Colonel Walter Blume. Graduated in law at University of Erlangen.

SS-Colonel Martin Sandberger. Studied jurisprudence at Universities of Munich, Freiburg, Cologne and Tuebinger. Assistant judge in Inner Administration of Wuerttemberg.

SS-Colonel Willy Seibert. Graduated from University of Goettingen in 1932 in economics.

SS-Colonel Eugen Steimle. Studied history, Germanic languages and French at the Universities of Tuebingen and Berlin.

Second Row:

SS-Colonel Ernst Biberstein. Former clergyman.

92

SS-Colonel Werner Braune. Graduated in law from University of Jena and obtained degree of Doctor of Juridical Science.

SS-Lieutenant Colonel Walter Haensch. Studied law at Leipzig University and trained as "Referendar."

SS-Lieutenant Colonel Gustav Nosske. Studied banking, economics and law. Became assessor and "entered Administration of Justice" at Halle.

SS-Lieutenant Colonel Adolf Ott. Began career in administrative office of German Workers' front in Lindau.

SS-Lieutenant Colonel Eduard Strauch. Graduate Erlangen University. Member Intelligence service, press officer, disciplinary officer general SS.

SS-Major Woldemar Klingelhoefer. Voice teacher and opera singer.

SS-Major Lothar Fendler. Doctor in dentistry.

SS-Major Waldemar Von Radetzky. Linguist. Worked with import firm.

SS-Captain Felix Ruehl. Commercial Clerk. Lived in England for one year.

SS-First Lieutenant Heinz Hermann Schubert. High School education; apprentice to lawyer and "registrator." In civil administrative service.

SS-Master Sergeant Mathias Graf. Independent business man and civil servant.

When Brigadier General Telford Taylor addressed the Tribunal he described the defendants in vivid language. "These defendants are not German peasants or artisans drafted into the Wehrmacht. They are not uneducated juveniles. They are lawyers, teachers, artists, and a former clergyman. They are, in short, men of education, who

93

were in full possession of their faculties and who fully understood the grave and sinister significance of the program they embarked upon. They were part of the hard core of the SS. They did not give mere lip service to Himmler's atrocious racial doctrines; they were chosen for this terrible assignment because they were thought to be men of sufficient ruthlessness to carry them out. They are hand-picked fanatics; every one of them was an officer of the SS . . . They are not unhappy victims, unwillingly pushed into crime by the tyranny of the Third Reich; these men, above all others, themselves, spread the Nazi doctrine with fire and sword."

As one studied the defendants, a common facial characteristic emerged—an undeviating expression of resolution, a firmness of purpose which once carried them through thousands of miles of territory on as relentless an expedition as ever spurred human endeavor, and which now was devoted to as serious a project as could ever engage a human being, that of saving their necks. With the cloud of murder charges, there hung over every defendant an invisible noose and, at the same time, an invisible white cloak of exoneration. Which of these was to drop depended to a great extent on what the defendant would say and what would be said by his lawyer.

The twenty-three defense lawyers, all wearing black robes, the European attorney's court dress, sat in front of the dock at tables piled high with documents and law books. They were very attentive and extremely deferential to the judges. If one left the courtroom during the session, he always stopped at the door until he got the attention of the presiding judge, and then he bowed from the waist in homage before departing.

Behind the dock stood six American soldiers in neat olive-drab uniforms wearing Eisenhower jackets and

94

gleaming helmets. None carried firearms although the sergeant in charge held unostentatiously behind his back a white, highly polished round stick.

To the right of the defense lawyers sat the prosecution attorneys at tables of their own. To the rear of the prosecution tables extended seats for the press and spectators. A balcony accommodated a further visitors' gallery for a total of 350 seats.

Three large bronze plaques ornamented the walls: one represented human frailty in the form of Eve offering the apple to Adam; another was a winged hourglass portraying the fleeting nature of time; the third proclaimed the Ten Commandments. The doors were framed in heavy dark green marble. A white, silky light fell from long fluorescent tubes which suggested open skylights. Sage green curtains hung over the windows. With whitewashed upper walls, dark brown paneling and wine-colored chairs, the courtroom projected dignity and was worthy of the epochal work to be done in it.

At the center of a long table in, front of the judges' bench sat Colonel John E. Ray, Secretary General of the Tribunal. On either side were court clerks and court reporters, the latter recording in English and in translated German every word being uttered by Mr. Ferencz.

A brilliant young lawyer, a graduate of the Harvard Law School, enjoying a perfect command of the German language, and armed with a rough-and-ready military experience gained as a member of an American combat outfit in Germany during the war, Benjamin Ferencz was excellently equipped to study and evaluate the Einsatzgruppen reports. It was Brigadier General Telford Taylor who had assigned this young man to the task of analyzing the captured documents, drafting the indictment, locating the accused men in the various Prisoner of War com-

95

pounds, selecting assistant trial lawyers, taking an active part in the trial work and generally supervising the entire prosecution.

Counsel for the prosecution were assisted in preparing the case by Walter H. Rapp (Chief of the Evidence Division), Rolf Wartenberg and Alfred Schwarz, interrogators, and Nancy Fenstermacher and Charles E. Ippen, research and documentary analysts.

The mammoth preliminary labors having been accomplished, Mr. Ferencz now addressed the Tribunal: "May it please your Honors. Vengeance is not our goal, nor do we seek merely a just retribution. We ask this Court to affirm by international penal action man's right to live in peace and dignity regardless of his race or creed. The case we present is a plea of humanity to law."

Then, after a pause and a glance which took in the whole courtroom and particularly the twenty-three Einsatzgruppen officers, he continued.

"Each of the defendants in the dock held a position of responsibility or command in an extermination unit. Each assumed the right to decide the fate of men, and death was the intended result of his power and contempt. Their own reports will show that the slaughter committed by these defendants was dictated, not by military necessity, but by that supreme perversion of thought, the Nazi theory of the master race. We shall show that these deeds of men in uniform were the methodical execution of long-range plans to destroy ethnic, national, political, and religious groups which stood condemned in the Nazi mind."

Mr. Ferencz spoke for about forty-five minutes and then called on Assistant Prosecution Counsel Peter W. Walton to continue with the opening presentation. Walton, some forty years of age, with gray touching his temples and with a slight pleasant drawl which confirmed the biographical note that he was born in Georgia, carried forward the harrowing chronicle. He explained that the Einsatzgruppen organization was made up of four groups, each group consisting of from five hundred to eight hundred men.

"These small forces totaling not more than three thousand men killed at least one million human beings in approximately two years' time. These figures enable us to make estimates which help considerably in understanding this case. They show that the four Einsatzgruppen averaged some 1,350 murders per day during a two-year period; 1,350 human beings slaughtered on the average day, seven days a week for more than one hundred weeks . . . All these thousands of men, women, and children killed had first to be selected, brought together, held in restraint, and transported to a place of death. They had to be counted, stripped of possessions, shot, and buried. And burial did not end the job, for all of the pitiful possessions taken from the dead had to be salvaged, crated, and shipped to the Reich. Finally, books were kept to cover these transactions. Details of all these things had to be recorded and reported."

Ferencz had divided the prosecution trial work among four lawyers. He had himself taken the responsibility of presenting the evidence against the defendants who belonged to Einsatzgruppe B, and Walton was to handle Einsatzgruppe D. John E. Glancey was to prosecute the members of Einsatzgruppe A and Arnost Horlik-Hochwald Einsatzgruppe C. John E. Glancey was as different in appearance from Arnost Horlik-Hochwald as their respective birthplaces were geographically distant from each other. Glancey, born and reared in Washington, D.C., was tall and broad-shouldered, and looked like a football player. Arnost Horlik-Hochwald, born in Czech-

97

oslovakia, could be visualized only in an intellectual setting. Of medium height with a shock of gray hair and wearing glasses with thick lenses, he was soft-spoken, polite and extremely courteous. He served in his home country's army during the war and then, as a member of the Czechoslovakian delegation to the United Nations War Crimes Commission, came to Nuremberg. Here General Taylor and Mr. Ferencz obtained his services as a trial lawyer and assigned him to the Einsatzgruppen case.

James E. Heath of South Carolina was listed as a consultant in the case, and was especially assigned to cross-examine Ohlendorf, the Number One defendant.

CHAPTER SIX

WHEN MR. FERENCZ STATED TO THE TRIBUNAL THAT HE would prove the defendants had killed one million persons, the resulting impression in the courtroom was that he was dealing more or less in abstract figures. The evidence soon suggested otherwise. One report stated casually that in order to get the program started in a certain ghetto "there would be executions of a minor nature of fifty to one hundred persons."

Another report (No. 55) speaking of operations in the oblast of N. Kaliningrad, Russia, said that in Audrini, "on 2 January [1942] at the order of Einsatzgruppe A, the village was completely burnt down after removal of all foodstuffs, etc., and all the villagers shot." Then in the neighboring town of Rossiten, "301 men were publicly shot in the market square . . . All these actions were carried out without incident."

I wondered how men could become so hardened to brutality that they could raze a town and destroy the population of two towns, and not regard such destructive fury as even an "incident."

But even with killings of three hundred here and sev-

99

eral hundred there, it still seemed impossible that the total number of corpses could stretch out to the ungraspable figure of one million. However, when the reports came in describing the execution of thousands and tens of thousands, one saw, as a glimpse over a limitless sea of tombstones, that in speaking of one million murders Mr. Ferencz had not been engaging in figures of speech but in numerals of cast iron reality. Einsatzgruppe A, reporting its activities in Latvia up to October 15, 1941, said: "Up to now, 30,000 Jews were executed in all."

Einsatzgruppe B, operating in the direction of Moscow, reported that in the month of October, 1941 "the liquidations of 37,180 people took place."

Einsatzgruppe C, reporting some 51,000 executions from the wheat-growing regions of the Ukraine, announced the reasons behind the killings: "These were the motives for the executions carried out by the Kommandos: Political officials, looters and saboteurs, active Communists and political representatives, Jews who gained their release from prison camps by false statements, agents and informers of the NKWD, persons who, by false depositions and influencing witnesses, were instrumental in the deportation of ethnic Germans, Jewish sadism and revengefulness, undesirable elements, partisans, politrucks, dangers of plague and epidemics, members of Russian bands, armed insurgents . . . provisioning of Russian bands, rebels and agitators, drifting juveniles . . ." and then came the all inclusive phrase: "Jews in general."

The summary execution of random collections of human beings described as "drifting juveniles" and of groups so vaguely generalized as "undesirable elements" startlingly revealed how indistinct was the limit of the sweep of the Einsatzgruppen's deadly scythe. The reference in the reports to individual categories of Jews, such as "Jews

100

who gained their release from prison camps by false statements," was of course only grisly window dressing because under the heading "Jews in general," all Jews were killed regardless of antecedents.

The writer of Operational Report No. 190, reciting the activities of Ohlendorf's Einsatzgruppe D, stated that, in the second half of March, 1942, a total of 1,501 people were executed and then added in a commonplace manner, "Total number shot up to date, 91,678."

Although the Einsatz executioners (following instructions from Adolf Eichmann) were tight-lipped about their deeds, it was impossible to muffle the echoes of their rifles; and the grapevine telegraph buzzed with horrible stories which would not down. The leader of Einsatz-kommando 5 in Uman, a railroad terminus south of Kiev, complained to Amt IV, B4 that the army authorities had been lax in allowing soldiers to talk. As a consequence, Jews were forewarned and fled the city. "Reports about actions against Jews gradually filter through from fleeing Jews, Russians, and also from unguarded talk of German soldiers." The escaping Jews, however, were recaptured and executed with populations in adjoining towns, so that the Kommando could report, "Altogether, 75,881 persons have been executed."

Activity and Situation Report No. 9, covering January, 1942, apprised Amt. IV, B4, that "In White Ruthenia the purge of Jews is in full swing. The number of Jews in the Territory handed over to the Civil authorities up to now amounts to 139,000. 33,210 Jews were shot meanwhile by the Einsatzgruppen of the Security Police and the SD."

Reporting on August 10, 1942, the Commissioner General for the area involved specified that "In the city of Minsk, about 10,000 Jews were liquidated on 28 and 29

July, 6,500 of whom were Russian Jews—mainly old people, women and children—the remainder consisted of Jews unfit for work."

But the Commissioner General was not satisfied with conditions in Baranowitschi and Hanzewitschi. He said that in the former city there were about ten thousand Jews "still living in the town alone." He announced that "radical measures still remain to be taken," and he would take those radical measures. He promised that nine thousand would be "liquidated next month." Why he held over the remaining thousand until the following month he did not divulge.

Like election returns, the figures on executions came pouring into Eichmann's office in Berlin, and with the characteristic Teutonic precision and passion for orderliness the reports were duly mimeographed and tabulated, copies were distributed and originals filed. Then when the war suddenly terminated, Eichmann changed from his gaudy SS black uniform into an ordinary enlisted man's uniform, adopted another name and went into hiding. While the Central Intelligence Agency looked for him throughout Europe in all the prisoner of war camps, displaced persons camps and refugee settlements, Allied soldiers came upon his most prized treasure—the documentary evidence of what he had done to the Jews. The reports were covered with the dust of debris but the printing was as clear as the story they related was grim. In due time the reports appeared in Nuremberg—under circumstances the Einsatzgruppen leaders had never expected to face.

The reports are appallingly enlightening. Although from a statistical point of view there is not much purpose in citing them further, we cannot omit one report made by Einsatzgruppe A on October 15, 1941. After announcing that 71,105 Jews had been executed in Lithuania, the Einsatz commander appended an inventory of all persons killed by his organization, just as a business house might notify its main office of the business done to date. The inventory read:

"Total:	Jews	Communists	Total
Lithuania	80,311	860	81,171
Latvia	30,025	1,845	31,868
Esthonia	474	684	1,158
White Ruthenia	7,620	——	7,620
	118,430	3,387	121,817

to be added to these figures:

In Lithuania and Latvia Jews annihilated by pogroms	5,500
Jews, Communists and partisans executed in old-Russian area	2,000
Lunatics executed	748
(correct total 130,065)	122,455
Communists and Jews liquidated by State Pol. and Security Service Tilsit during search actions	5,502
	135,567"

And so, under clear skies and dark skies, in the flowering spring and while autumn leaves were falling, in the bright sunshine and in the deep snow, the Einsatzgruppen continued to reap their red harvest, while the adding machines in Eichmann's headquarters clicked noisily into the night, totaling the figures the Kommando leaders transmitted by wireless, mail, and courier.

Farmers in their rough corduroys and jeans, fishermen with the scent of the sea in their oilskins, mechanics in overalls reeking with grease, shoemakers smelling of wax and leather, carpenters trailing sawdust, lawyers bereft

103

of brief cases and papers, doctors torn from hospitals and operating tables, clerks with wilted collars and shiny sleeves, peasant women with shawls about their heads, old ladies and old men leaning on crutches and canes, young girls rosy with health and promise, children laughing, crying, whimpering—all crowded into trucks careening toward that one rendezvous: the anti-tank ditches in the woods.

Of course, no human brain can grasp the reality of one million deaths, because life, the supreme essence of consciousness and being, does not lend itself to complete realistic evaluation. Life is so beyond mental comprehension that only its destruction offers a infinitesimal suggestion of its incalculable worth. The loss of any one person can only begin to be measured in the numbing realization by surviving kin and friends that he is gone forever. The extermination, therefore, of one million human beings is beyond one's capacity to feel. One cannot even begin to calculate the full cumulative terror of murder one million times repeated.

In an attempt to grasp the enormity of the Einsatzgruppen operation, one must try not to visualize one million murders, but perhaps a family of eight persons falling before Einsatz gunfire. Herman Friedrich Graebe, who related the pogrom which occurred in Sdolbunow, Ukraine, witnessed such an execution. He described the scene of the extermination of such a small family as it stood out in heart-rending bas-relief in the midst of a Kommando massacre on October 5, 1943, at Dubno, Ukraine:

> Moennikes and I went direct to the pits. Nobody bothered us. Now I heard rifle shots in quick succession, from

behind one of the earth mounds. The people who had got off the trucks—men, women and children of all ages—had to undress upon the orders of an SS-man, who carried a riding or dog whip.

They had to put down their clothes in fixed places, sorted according to shoes, top clothing and underclothing. I saw a heap of shoes of about 800 to 1,000 pairs, great piles of underlinen and clothing. Without screaming or weeping these people undressed, stood around in family groups, kissed each other, said farewells and waited for a sign from another SS-man, who stood near the pit, also with a whip in his hand.

During the 15 minutes that I stood near the pit I heard no complaint or plea for mercy. I watched a family of about 8 persons, a man and woman, both about 50 with their children of about 1, 8 and 10, and two grown up daughters of about 20 to 24. An old woman with snow-white hair was holding the one year old child in her arms and singing to it, and tickling it. The child was cooing with delight. The couple were looking on with tears in their eyes. The father was holding the hand of a boy about 10 years old and speaking to him softly; the boy was fighting his tears. The father pointed toward the sky, stroked his head, and seemed to explain something to him. At that moment the SS-man at the pit shouted something to his comrade.

I looked into the pit and saw that the bodies were twitching or the heads lying already motionless on top of the bodies that lay before them. Blood was running from their necks. I was surprised that I was not ordered away, but I saw that there were two or three postmen in uniform nearby. The next batch was approaching already.

CHAPTER SEVEN

ON SEPTEMBER 15, 1947, THE DAY OF ARRAIGNMENT, ONE of the most remarkable persons ever to appear before the public gaze stepped into the Nuremberg courtroom. Handsome, poised, suave and polite, he carried himself with the bearing of a person endowed with natural dignity and intellect, and, in the course of his testimony, he was to display the narrative talents of a professional raconteur. Forty years of age, slender and with delicate features and neatly combed dark brown hair, he looked out at the world through penetrating blue-gray eyes. His voice was excellently modulated, his hands well-shaped and carefully groomed, and he moved gracefully and self-confidently. The only blemish in the perfection of his personality was that he had killed ninety thousand people.

This disclosure, although not entirely incapable of producing some horror among even the most stouthearted, did not detract from his distinctiveness; if anything, it added to it. Visitors, even before they got seated, craned their necks in the direction of the prisoners' dock, and, although warned by guards against pointing, invariably thrust an index finger in Otto Ohlendorf's direction, asking if he was the ninety thousand murderer. Women crowded into the courtroom to marvel at him and some even sought to pass him notes offering encouragement and endearment.

Participants in and viewers of the international war crimes trials generally agreed that, next to Herman Goering, Otto Ohlendorf stood out as the most compelling personality of all the defendants. With Hjalmar Schacht, the fabulous Nazi minister of finance, he achieved the highest IQ rating among the Nuremberg prisoners. Born in Hanover, a graduate of the Leipzig and Goettingen universities, a lecturer in political science, Ohlendorf early hitched his wagon to the Hitler star, and, by demonstrated ability in the Nazi organization, won rapid promotion. He was only thirty-four when his friend Eichmann recommended him as leader of Einsatzgruppe D, with the rank of major general in the all-powerful Schutzstaffeln, popularly known as the Elite Guard or SS.

The electric sensation of absolute authority which accompanies military rank never deserted the young major-general so that even in the courtroom Ohlendorf wore— as undoubtedly he would carry to his grave—the invisible epaulets before which so much of the world had once bowed and scraped in deference, homage and fear.

Even after the German forces had surrendered, but he was not yet a prisoner, he discussed with Himmler whether he should give himself up. This episode narrated by him in court on October 8, 1947, caused me to ask, "But when you say that on the ninth of May you were discussing whether you should go over to the Allies, this was like the mouse discussing whether he should go over to the cat. You had already surrendered."

But he did not regard himself as having surrendered

since there was still an existing German government at Flensburg. Thus, standing on his dignity as an official of that government and as an officer of the SS, he asked the Allies to arrest him. He had to ask three times.

"When was that? What date?"

"That was on the twenty-third of May."

"Then they favored you by arresting you."

And, without a smile, he replied, "Yes, on the twenty-third of May."

As a defendant, Ohlendorf, like Goering, staged a performance which would have stirred theater audiences on either side of the ocean. No detail of the trial escaped him. He sat intense over every controverted piece of evidence, grimaced when things went badly, smiled when the testimony pleased him, scolded his lawyer when he seemed lacking in aggressiveness, and uttered audible disgust when any of his fellow defendants fumbled on the witness stand. To the judges he was amiable and polite. Each morning as he entered the dock he ceremoniously bowed to the bench, and each evening he smiled a benign *auf Wiedersehen* as he departed for his prison cell to sleep on his pallet, unhaunted, without doubt, by dreams of the multitudes he had slain.

He flickered not an eyelash as Prosecutor Peter Walton charged that Ohlendorf's unit "killed at an average rate of 340 per day," but that "between 16 November and 15 December 1941, this Einsatzgruppe killed an average of 700 human beings per day for the whole 30-day period."

On the witness stand Ohlendorf, in justifying these killings, essayed varying roles of histrionic projection. At times he could have been a Hamlet, wrapped in deep thought and meditation, and at other times he slashed out boldly, a Macbeth staking all on daring and self-

108

assurance of ultimate victory. Rhetorical sparks flew as he crossed and clashed blades with prosecution counsel, to the delight of his admiring co-defendants. Of the twenty-three accused men, Ohlendorf stood out as the Number One defendant, not only because of his end seat in the dock but mainly because of his undisputed intellectual superiority and coolheadedness. Only on one score did his brother defendants fear and distrust him: Ohlendorf was mathematically honest. And if they were to follow his example and admit to statistical slayings, as Ohlendorf unflinchingly conceded he had put ninety thousand to eternal rest, how could they expect exoneration?

With flung-back shoulders and the confident voice of the architect who might have superintended the construction of the Egyptian pyramids, Ohlendorf related from the witness stand, while sipping at a glass of water, how, at the head of Einsatzgruppe D, he followed the Nazi troops which had overcome enemy opposition, through Bessarabia and the Crimean peninsula, carrying out the genocidal orders of his lord and master, Adolf Hitler.

He did not like to do all this, he explained with the air of a conscientious parent who must discipline an unruly child. He said it was his duty. And then, pitching his voice in a self-pitying tone, he said, "There is nothing worse for people spiritually than to have to shoot defenseless populations."

But his bid for commiseration and vindication fell on deaf ears so far as cross-examining Prosecutor James E. Heath was concerned. "There is nothing worse than to be shot either," Heath sardonically remarked, "when you are defenseless."

Ohlendorf, however, was not to be outdone. "I can

imagine worse things," he rasped, "for example, to starve."
Heath rose from the prosecution table and confronted the
defendant. With his headphones he seemed even taller
than six feet. Ohlendorf, wearing the same type of gear,
became a still more awesome figure than his actual words
made him. The translated dialogue poured into the headphones from the interpreters sitting behind a glass barrier at the side of the prisoners' enclosure and no time
was lost. The questions and answers bounded back and
forth with the speed and bounce of tennis balls, and the
translation was so fluent that the listener quickly forgot
the principals were not talking the same language.

Ohlendorf's victims were mainly Jews but he killed
gypsies also. "On what basis did you kill gypsies?" Heath
asked.

"It is the same as for the Jews," Ohlendorf replied.

Since the Nazis had proclaimed the theory of a master
race, Heath now put the whole ironic projection of that
theory into a one-word question: "Blood?"

Ohlendorf answered, "I think I can add up from my
own knowledge of European history that the Jews actually
during wars regularly carried on espionage service on
both sides."

Heath looked up to me, as if to inquire whether the
translating machinery was working properly, because he
was asking about gypsies and Ohlendorf continued to
talk about Jews. I directed Ohlendorf to the subject of
Heath's questioning. With a disparaging gesture of his
hand, Ohlendorf answered, "There was no difference between gypsies and Jews. At the time the same order
existed for the Jews. I added the explanation that it is
known from European history that the Jews actually
during all wars carried out espionage service on both
sides."

I reminded the defendant again: "Well, now, what we

are trying to do is to find out what you are going to say about the gypsies, but you still insist on going back to the Jews, and Mr. Heath is questioning about gypsies. Is it also in European history that gypsies always participated in political strategy and campaigns?"

Ohlendorf was pleased to open up the history books. "The gypsies in particular. I want to draw your recollection to extensive descriptions of the Thirty-Year War by Ricardo, Huck and Schiller——"

Since the Thirty Years' War was fought in 1618-48, I could not help interrupting. "That is going back pretty far in order to justify the killing of gypsies in 1941, isn't it?

This suggestion that he was giving a three-hundred-year motivation to his death-dealing enterprise did not ruffle the ex-SS Major General. "I added that as an explanation, as such motive might have had a part in this, to get at this decision."

What was the real purpose behind the killing of Jews and gypsies? Ohlendorf was almost annoyed at questions of this character. Why, it was a matter of self-defense, he explained in the tone of one who is wasting time explaining that the earth is round. The Jews posed a continuous danger for the German occupation troops. Moreover, they could some day attack Germany proper, and self-preservation dictated their destruction before they began an aggressive march on Berlin.

Heath was not impressed with this argument. Assume that the Jews in Bessarabia, the Crimea and the Ukraine could one day shoulder guns against the Germans, he said; assume that their wives could help them—but what about the Jewish children, the gypsy children? Heath thundered his question at Ohlendorf.

Ohlendorf imperturbably replied, "According to orders they were to be killed just like their parents."

Heath walked away from the witness stand to control

111

his anger at the casualness with which Ohlendorf had made this shocking revelation. Then turning swiftly on his heel he fired again at the defendant: "Will you explain to the Tribunal what conceivable threat to the security of the Wehrmacht [armed forces] a child constituted in your judgment?"

Ohlendorf answered in staccatoed accents, amazed that Heath should still linger on the subject. "I believe I cannot add anything to your previous question. I did not have to determine the danger but the order contained that all Jews including the children were considered to constitute a danger for the security of this area."

But Heath did not let up. "Will you agree that there was absolutely no rational basis for killing children except genocide and the killing of races?"

The atmosphere of the courtroom filled with electric tension. Many spectators lifted their hands to their headsets, pressing on the earpads as if to increase the volume of sound so as not to lose a word of the reply which they anticipated would be momentous. Their nervous expectations were fulfilled as Ohlendorf delivered the answer which set off a murmur of horror. "I believe that it is very simple to explain if one starts from the fact that this order did not only try to achieve a [temporary] security but also a permanent security because for that reason the children were people who would grow up and surely being the children of parents who had been killed they would constitute a danger no smaller than that of the parents."*

Heath caught his breath and launched on another subject of cross-examination. However, the tautness of his

* The defendant Erwin Schulz also stated: "Jewish women and children were, if necessary, to be shot as well, in order to prevent acts of revenge."

features clearly told that he was still concerned about Ohlendorf's explanation. It was as perfect a piece of logic as could be found in Aristotle, but it was too perfect. There had to be a flaw somewhere, so Heath returned to the bewitchingly macabre subject:

"To come back to the question of murder and the children of the slaughtered in Russia. I think you have not yet answered my question. What conceivable threat to the Wehrmacht was offered by the children of gypsies and Jews, let's say under five years of age?"

Ohlendorf said he had already answered that query, and so for Heath's benefit I summed up Ohlendorf's explanation: "The witness has stated that the reason these children under five, under four, under three, down to conception I image, were killed is that they were a possible threat to Germany in the future years. That is his answer and he stands on it."

But Ohlendorf had not been entirely without heart. There was one feature about massacring the children which had grated on his tender sensibilities. Some of his men were married and had children. Ohlendorf had five of his own. As the executioners looked at the helpless tots framed within the sights of their rifles they often thought of their little boys and girls at home and sometimes aimed badly. Then, the Kommando or platoon leader had to go about with revolver or carbine, firing into the screaming and writhing creatures on the ground. This was all quite unmilitary. Then, also, many of the riflemen missed their targets when they had to kill women because they thought of wives, daughters, sisters and mothers far away.

Adolf Eichmann found a way out of the awkward situation. He provided for gas vans which would save the sentimental assassins from too much suffering. These vehicles resembled family trailers. Painted windows adorned the sides, frescoed curtains seemed to flap in the breeze, the image of a flower pot on the image of a window sill added to the charming deception. The attractive looking autocars rolled up to the groups of waiting mothers and children who were told that they were to be taken to their husbands and fathers. Ohlendorf described the procedure: "One could not see from the van what purpose it had, and the people were told that they were being moved, and therefore they entered without hesitation."

Thus, joyfully, the women clambered aboard, holding by the hand or in their arms their babies, some laughing, some crying, but everyone excited over the trip which was to take them away from hardship and persecution, to begin life anew in another land by the side and under the protection of their strong men folk who had already gone ahead to prepare the happy way for them.

As soon as the unsuspecting pilgrims entered the vehicle, the doors slammed shut, automatically and hermetically. The driver tramped on the accelerator; monoxide gas streamed into the interior. The women screamed as their children toppled to the floor or succumbed in their arms, but before they could rescue them or breathe encouragement, the deadly vapor had entered their own lungs; and soon the moving van had become a traveling mortuary. By the time the van reached its destination—a long deep ditch outside the town—all the occupants were dead. And here they joined the husbands and fathers who had already preceded them into the "new land" via the sub-machine guns and rifles of that astonishing organization known as the Einsatzgruppen.

Ohlendorf was asked how long it would take to execute persons by the use of these lethal gas vans after they

114

were subjected to gas. The ex-general lifted his hand to his forehead as if trying to assist the machinery of recollection. It was a detail of which apparently he had never made a mental note. At last he lowered his hand and said, "As far as I remember, about ten minutes."

Sometimes there were more demands for the gas vans than Ohlendorf could supply but he was equal to every emergency. Thus, "If there were three requisitions we would send the two cars to the two kommandos who had the largest number of prospects. But that was done in a very simple, businesslike manner."

To the Einsatzgruppen, everything was quite businesslike about these ghastly vehicles of death. Communications between Eichmann's headquarters and Einsatzgruppen commanders in the field spoke of gas wagons with the casualness of correspondence on coal trucks. Nor, in keeping with the German passion for maintaining records, was there documentation lacking on this awesome subject. In the innumerable filing cabinets found in the Gestapo headquarters appeared copies of letters, invoices, repair bills, etc., having to do with the gas vans. One letter from the Security Police and Security Service Ostland to Amt IV, B4, dated June 15, 1942, asked for the immediate shipment of one five-ton van and twenty gas hoses to take the place of some leaky ones in order that there might be no delay in the treatment of Jews "in a special way."

In a letter, dated May 16, 1942, SS-Unstersturmfuehrer Becker made a practical recommendation with regard to the operation of the lethal device. He said that many of the drivers failed to apply the gas properly. "In order to come to an end as fast as possible, the driver presses the accelerator to the fullest extent. By doing that the persons to be executed suffer death from suffocation and

115

not death by dozing off as planned. My directions have now proved that by correct adjustment of the levers death comes faster and the prisoners fall asleep peacefully."

Eichmann, who had taken a course in engineering at school in Linz, looked into the "levers" situation and found no mechanical defect. He decided that all that was necessary in order to obtain maximum results from the gas vans was for the drivers to be given special instructions. Accordingly he set up a school for that purpose.

The vans themselves were constructed in Berlin and driven under their own power to the fields of action. It would be interesting to speculate on the thoughts of the drivers as they rolled through half of Europe, traversing city and country, climbing mountains and penetrating plains, traveling over a thousand miles with their gaseous guillotines to kill women they had never seen and children they could never know.

While the gas van had its advantages in that it brought death to women and children without the executioners' having to look them in the eye, it still did not prove to its users to be a faultless engine for human destruction. When the execution was accomplished by shooting, the job was quickly finished, since the bodies fell into the already dug graves. But the gas vans presented the job of removing the corpses and then burying them. Traces of the gas still remained and the mass of tumbled bodies produced a problem of its own. The executioners complained of headaches. As Becker worded the complaint in an official report, the unloading process inflicted "immense psychological injuries and damage to the health" of the unloaders.

Ohlendorf maintained a physician on his staff to treat the "psychological injuries" and to supervise the health

116

of his men generally. Occasionally the physician was used as an expert to determine if the people in the gas vans were dead before burial but this precaution was really unnecessary, Ohlendorf said, because he "had a look that the people died without any difficulties."

Ohlendorf insisted that throughout his entire Nazi career he was motivated only by the highest of ideals and ethics. This caused Heath to inquire whether he regarded Hitler's order against the Jews and others as justified in the realm of morals. "Was it morally right, or was it morally wrong?"

Ohlendorf replied that it was not for him to pass on Hitler's intentions.

"I do not ask you for a judgment of Hitler's morals; I ask you for an expression of your own moral conception. The question is not whether Hitler was moral; but what, in your moral judgment, was the character of this order: Was it a moral order, or an immoral order?"

Dauntless and as sure of himself as a Prussian field marshal on parade, Ohlendorf nevertheless perceived that a discussion on moral issues could make him appear something less than the Spartan, valorous executant of military orders which he said it was his duty to obey. Accordingly he repeated that it was not up to him to pass on the moral quality of Hitler's actions. Heath insisted that the question be answered and appealed to the Tribunal. I turned to Ohlendorf: "When this order was given to you to go out to kill, you had to appraise it, instinctively. The soldier who goes into battle knows that he must kill, but he understands that it is a question of battle with an equally armed enemy. But you were going out to shoot down defenseless people. Now, didn't the question of the morality of that order enter your mind? Let us suppose that the order had been—and I don't

117

mean any offense in this question—suppose the order had been that you kill your sister. Would you not have instinctively morally appraised that order as to whether it was right or wrong—morally, not politically or militarily—but as a matter of humanity, conscience, and justice?"

Ohlendorf moved slightly in the witness chair. His eyes roved about the courtroom; his hand opened and clenched convulsively. He was aware that a man who would kill his own sister made of himself something less than human. On the contrary, if he replied that he would refuse to execute such an order he would contradict his assertion that he had no choice in obeying his superior's command. Accordingly, he answered obliquely, "I am not in a position, your Honor, to isolate this occurrence from the others."

He sought a parallelism so as not to manifest alarm at the dilemma the question posed. He related how he saw many civilian Germans killed in Allied air raids and then declared, "I am not prepared, or in a position to give today a moral judgment about that order."

But Heath was not content to leave the subject dangling unresolved in midair. He pressed the question as to how Ohlendorf would respond to a direct order involving an obviously difficult assignment. "If you had received an order from Adolf Hitler to kill your own flesh and blood, would you have executed the order, or not?"

Ohlendorf parried the thrust. "I consider the question frivolous." But the question was far from frivolous for him. He actually had a sister, and two brothers, in addition to his five children.

Heath relentlessly pursued the query. "Then I understand you to say that if one person be involved in a killing order, a moral question arises, but if thousands of human

118

beings are involved, you can see no moral questions; it is a matter of numbers?"

Ohlendorf's pale features went parchment-white as he retorted angrily: "Mr. Prosecutor, I think you are the only one to understand my answer in this way, that it is not a matter of one single person, but from the point of departure events have happened in history which among other things have led to deeds committed in Russia, and such an historical process you want me to analyze in a moral way. I, however, refuse moral evaluation with good reasons as outlined, so far as my own conscience is concerned."

Heath continued and intensified the attack: "Suppose you found your sister in Soviet Russia, and your sister were included in that category of gypsies—not a Jewess but in a gypsy band—and she was brought before you for slaughter because of her presence in the gypsy band; what would have been your action? She is there in the process of history, which you have described."

Ohlendorf fought for time as with flashing eyes he signaled to his attorney to intervene. Dr. Aschenauer, tall, dark, and, in his long flowing black robe, looking something like a Shakespearean actor, rose dramatically and, echoing his client's defiance, declaimed, "I object to this question and I ask that it not be admitted. This is no question for cross-examination."

The prosecution insisted on a reply. Ohlendorf with his expressive countenance urged his attorney not to abandon his protest. Aschenauer lifted his berobed arm in challenge, and turned to the bench. "I ask for a ruling of the Tribunal upon my objection."

I conferred with my colleagues and we decided the defendant should be required to answer.

I explained to Ohlendorf that the question was of

119

course an extraordinary one and would not be tolerated in a trial other than one of this character where the defendant was confronted with the unprecedented charge of having murdered ninety thousand people. Under those circumstances the question was relevant because his answer would throw a light on his reaction to the Fuehrer-Order.

Ohlendorf was not convinced he should answer. I explained further that he admitted the Fuehrer-Order called for execution of defenseless people. "You will admit that in normal times such a proposition would be incredible and intolerable, but you claim that the circumstances were not normal, and, therefore, what might be accepted only with terrified judgment ordinarily, was accepted at that time as a normal discharge of duty." Under those circumstances I ruled that he should answer and I repeated Heath's question: "Suppose that in the discharge of this duty you had been confronted with the necessity of deciding whether to kill, among hundreds of unknown people, one whom you knew very well."

Ohlendorf reflected only for an instant and then, with a contemptuous glance at Heath, which seemed to say he was sweeping him aside, he announced to the world that under the circumstances described he would indeed shoot his sister: "If this demand would have been made to me under the same prerequisites, that is, within the framework of an order, which is absolutely necessary militarily, then I would have executed that order."

Although Ohlendorf would kill his sister if Hitler ordered him to do so, he explained that he had no different feeling with regard to shooting others. He bore animosity toward no one. "I never hated an opponent or any enemy, and I still do not do so today," he testified, as he lifted his eyes to the newspaper reporters in the press box

120

as if appealing to world opinion for confirmation of his moral scruples.

He killed Jews and gypsies because of their offenses in history, current and past, but he did not hate them. In fact, he even suggested that he felt some antipathy to Hitler's order which required him to kill unarmed civilians. This prompted the question, "Could you not have, after a certain period of time, tried to evade this order by sickness?"

He stiffened in the witness chair as if to emphasize the invisible epaulets on his shoulders. Was the presiding judge trying to insult him? "I would have betrayed my men if I had left this command," he remarked rather icily. Solicitous about the welfare of his men, he would have had no assurance that, if he left, his successor would have manifested a similar solicitude. And, with a rising voice full of pride and moral justification, he added: "Despite everything, I considered this my duty and I shall consider it today as much more valuable than the cheap applause which I could have won if I had at that time betrayed my men by simulating illness."

Later on, under further examination, Ohlendorf admitted that even before the trial he could foresee that he would be asked why he did not hide behind a pretended incapacitation in order to avoid doing what he said he did not wish to do. Thus, he had prepared his answer. However, astute as he was, his sharp brain did not save him from a far more committal answer when he was not expecting an incriminating question. If he had really been conscientiously disturbed about killing defenseless people, there were other ways for him to avoid the murderous job without simulating illness. His Einsatzgruppe operated in an area within the jurisdiction of the Eleventh German Army, with which he was under orders to cooperate. It appears that the army commander did not have too high a regard for SS officers and, as a consequence, difficulties arose between him and Ohlendorf. Relating the story of those difficulties, Ohlendorf said, "I was called to the Chief of Staff, Colonel Woehler, and he received me by saying that if the collaboration between the army and myself would not improve, he would ask for my dismissal in Berlin."

As he finished this rather extended narrative, I asked him: "Were you so under the command of the army that a recommendation from this officer to Berlin could have worked the dismissal which he threatened?"

His unequivocal answer was, "Immediately, yes."

And here Ohlendorf exploded his whole defense of compulsion. If he had really recoiled before the prospect of ordering execution squads to mow down innocent people, he could have simply declined to co-operate with the army and he would have been on his way home or to a different assignment. But this lofty-minded chief chose to be humiliated by the army rather than give up his coveted command of Einsatzgruppe D and its spectacular distinction of achieving ninety thousand murders. He was more interested in being held in high regard by his friend and patron, Adolf Eichmann, who occasionally visited him in the field, than he was concerned about the death of innocent human beings.

In addition to justifying infanticide on the basis of preventing future reprisals, Ohlendorf asserted that the Allied nations were not without blame in this respect since many German children had been killed in Allied air raids. To this argument, Heath retorted, "Do you attempt to draw a moral comparison between the bomber who drops bombs hoping that it will not kill children and yourself who shot children deliberately? Is that a fair moral comparison?"

Ohlendorf did not flinch from the question. "I cannot imagine that these planes which systematically covered a city that was a fortified city, square meter for square meter, with incendiaries and explosive bombs and again with phosphorous bombs, and this done from block to block, and then as I have seen it in Dresden likewise the squares where the civilian population had fled to—that these men could possibly hope not to kill . . . civilian population and . . . children."

Heath conceded the point. "I think there is truth in what you say, though I never saw it." But he emphasized that Ohlendorf had given only part of the grim picture. "Does it occur to you that when the German Wehrmacht drove into Poland without provocation and when you drove into Norway and when you drove into the Low Countries and when you crushed France and when you destroyed Belgrade, Yugoslavia, Greece—when you put Rumania, Bulgaria under your heel, and then attempted to destroy the Russian State, does it not occur to you that people resisting your tyranny stand on a higher moral level when they resort to the same horrible cruelties which you initiated in order to destroy your tyranny. Answer that, please."

Ohlendorf did not hesitate to answer. "You will understand that I look at the events of the war which you referred to, in a different way than you do." That was the crux of Ohlendorf's defense: he and the other SS men differed in their viewpoint from the rest of mankind. Ohlendorf refused to see that when war planes bomb a city within whose borders are located ammunition plants, factories, railroads and telegraph and wireless stations, the object is to wreck and destroy these facilities for the purpose of crippling the hostile military forces. Of course, in such an operation, it inevitably happens that nonmilitary as well as military persons are killed. This is a grave

123

but unavoidable corollary of battle action. But the civilians are not pin-pointed for extinction. The bomb is aimed at the railroad yards, and houses along the tracks are hit and many of their occupants killed. This is entirely different, in fact and in law, from an armed force's marching up to these same railroad tracks, entering those abutting houses, dragging out the men, women and children of a particular race and shooting them.

Ohlendorf sneered that anyone who used the atom bomb should condemn him for killing helpless citizens. "The fact that individual men killed civilians face to face is looked upon as terrible and is pictured as specially gruesome because the order was clearly given to kill these people. I cannot morally evaluate a deed any better, a deed which makes it possible, by pushing a button, to kill a much larger number of civilians, men, women and children, even to hurt them for generations than those deeds of individual people who for the same purpose, namely, to achieve the goal of the war, must shoot individual persons. I believe that the time will come to remove these moral differences in executions for the purposes of war . . ."

There is no doubt that the invention of atomic and hydrogen bombs, as well as guided missiles, have added preoccupation and worry to the human race, but the atom bombs dropped in World War II were still not aimed at ethnic groups. Like any other type of aerial bomb, they were used to overcome military resistance and hasten surrender.

Thus, as grave a military action as is an air bombardment, whether it be by conventional or by atomic methods, the one and only purpose of the bombing is to effect the capitulation of the bombed nation. If the nation surrenders, the bombing ceases and the killing terminates. Moreover, a city may completely escape bombing by declaring itself an open city. But where Einsatzgruppen forces were involved, the situation was entirely different. Even if a nation in which Jews lived hauled down its flag, the Jews were still killed as individuals. No defendant asserted that a German victory over the Allies would have ended the Jewish liquidation program.

Throughout the entire Einsatzgruppen trial the defense did not produce one item of evidence to show how the killing of Jews in any way subdued or abated the military strength of the enemy. It was not demonstrated how indiscriminate slaughter of unarmed human beings could shorten, or help in any to win, the war for Germany. The annihilation of men, women and children branded as "inferior" had no bearing on the military issues at all.

For instance, Ohlendorf justified the killing of Jews in Russia on the basis that "the number of Jews in the general population in Russia, in relation to their number in the higher administration was very, very small." He emphasized that in Crimea, "up to 90 per cent of the administrative and leading authoritative positions were occupied by Jews." Thus, "for us it was obvious that Jewry in Bolshevist Russia played a disproportionately important role." This was the identical argument advanced in Germany to strip Jews of citizenship and property and inflict a hundred other penalties which were not only illegal but barbaric. But Ohlendorf assuredly had no duty and certainly no right in Russia or elsewhere to equalize, by means of firing squads, the number of official positions between Jews and non-Jews, even if it were to be assumed—of which, of course, he had no precise knowledge—that his statistics were correct.

Many of the defendants said that they were told at Pretzsch and in Berlin that "the Jews" supported Bolshevism, and had to be killed on that account. But it was not proved that every Jew espoused Bolshevism, although, even if that were true, killing him for his political belief would still be murder. As the Einsatz forces stormed into cities, towns and villages, they carried no lists of Jews they were to slay. They could not even be sure who were Jews. Interpreters accompanied the Kommandos, but it was impossible for them to cope with the many languages and dialects they encountered. Thus, it cannot be doubted, considering the speed with which massacres were organized and accomplished, that countless non-Jews were killed with the Jews. Operational Situation Report U.S.S.R. No. 170, reporting as of February 18, 1942, stated that "the number of persons executed in Simferopol increased to almost 10,000 Jews, *about 300 more than the number of Jews registered.*" (Emphasis supplied.)

If one who was not actually a Jew was listed for extermination as a Jew, what chance did he have to establish his Aryan genealogy? Writing on this subject to the defendant SS-Lieutenant Colonel Eduard Strauch, Heydrich said:

> Many of the Jews listed in your register are already known for continually trying to deny that they belong to the Jewish race by all possible and impossible reasons. It is, on the whole, in the nature of the matter that half-breeds of the first degree in particular try at every opportunity to deny that they are Jews.
>
> You will agree that in the third year of the war, there are matters of more importance for the war effort, and for the Security Police and the Security Service as well, than worrying about the wailing of Jews, making tedious investigations and preventing so many of my co-workers from other and much more important tasks.

126

CHAPTER EIGHT

GERMAN MILITARY DISCIPLINE HAS BEEN UNIVERSALLY accepted as the highest expression of undeviating obedience to superior orders. It has been said that a German soldier must obey orders, even though the heavens fall. The statement has become legendary. The Einsatzgruppen trial established how much this legend is based on fact and how much of it is sheer myth. SS-Lieutenant Colonel Willy Seibert, deputy to Ohlendorf, relied on the legend, and his attorney, Dr. Gawlik, banked on it. Taking the witness stand in his behalf, Seibert briskly described the military set-up which absolved him from all responsibility for the killings charged to him. Wearing a blue suit with broad pin stripes and looking like an overdressed, overpaid floorwalker, he expressed great surprise and even a mild indignation, under the examination of his attorney, that he should be required to account for any of the massacres conducted by his command. Then, under the cross-examination of Assistant Prosecutor Walton, he even went so far as to say that he did not know where murder started and where murder ended.

"Colonel, during your studies, particularly your studies

for the officer's examination, in your career in the Army and the SD, did you ever learn of the recognized rules and customs of war?"

"Of course."

"Have you, in your career, ever heard of the Geneva and Hague Conventions?"

"Yes."

"Did you not know that Germany was a signatory power to both these Conventions?"

"Yes, I knew that."

"Also, wasn't it known to you from your studies that the killing of civilians in occupied areas without trial is considered by international law and the laws of recognized warfare to be murder?"

"I cannot reply to that, Mr. Prosecutor, because I simply don't know where murder starts and murder ends."

This answer caused me to wonder whether he actually believed that he was safe under the theory of Superior Orders, or whether he had become so inured to bloodletting that he saw no moral or legal distinction between the killing in battle of an armed foe and the killing of an unresisting, unarmed civilian. Since it was the responsibility of our Tribunal to pass upon the facts as well as the law, we thus functioned as jury as well as judges. In European continental procedure, which was the only system known to the defendants and their lawyers, the presiding judge himself conducts most of the questioning of the accused and witnesses. It therefore became my duty to question Seibert, at length if necessary, in order to ascertain from him, to the extent that it was possible, just what was his concept of coercion under superior orders. I asked him, "Do you intend to have the Tribunal understand that you were unable to distinguish between murder and lawful killing?"

He replied that this was a question he could not answer "at the moment."

Suppose, I asked him, he saw a half dozen SS men kill a Jewish child in the Crimea, basing their action on an order which had been issued by Hitler. Would he call that murder?

He replied that this would be "killing by order," and therefore, in his opinion, "it is not murder."

Attorney Dr. Hans Gawlik stepped in to help his client.

"Witness, do you remember a maxim of a German Kaiser concerning the execution of orders by soldiers?"

"I don't know whether it was William the First or William the Second, but anyhow one Kaiser, Emperor, used the expression 'If the military situation or the entire situation makes it necessary, a soldier has to execute an order even if he would have to shoot at his own parents.'"

I asked the defendant if he subscribed to that doctrine. Much to the surprise of everyone in the courtroom he said he could not answer the question. The faces of the other defendants in the dock dropped. "Why, you idiot," they seemed to say, "*that* is our whole case."

I suggested to Seibert that he ought to answer the question since his own attorney had introduced the subject. He nervously tugged at the lapel of his coat and began throwing distress signals to Dr. Gawlick, but the latter was obviously as disturbed as the defendant who now found himself in a situation similar to the one which had confronted Ohlendorf when he was asked whether he would shoot his sister. Seibert, however, did not have Ohlendorf's skill, nor did he boast Ohlendorf's verbal audacity. In addition, he fretted that it was his own attorney who had impaled him on the horns of a dilemma which compelled him either to admit he would be inhuman enough to shoot his own parents or abandon the defense that he had no choice but to obey superior orders.

"Do you agree with it, or not? Do you agree with that statement which Dr. Gawlik asked you to quote?"

"Your Honor, I cannot answer this in so isolated a manner. If the military situation requires it, or some special situation—it can come to that."

"Then you agree with the William who issued that statement?"

"I don't want to say that. I only understand it to the effect, your Honor, that if regarded by a foreigner—the exaggerated importance of an order is conveyed to him."

"Well, this emperor was a German, wasn't he?"

"Yes."

"William the First, or William the Second?"

"Yes."

"And he made this statement?"

"According to my memory, yes."

"Well, is anyone authorized to assume that he was telling the truth, and that he meant what he said?"

"Your Honor, it cannot have been meant that somebody would have found himself in the situation to shoot his parents at some time in the near future."

"Then the first William or the second did not mean what he said?"

"I cannot say personally what he meant exactly, but in my opinion . . ."

"Now you tell me what you mean by it. Do you accept it or not?"

"I, myself, regard this declaration merely for expressing to the soldiers what significance an order has to the troops and that obedience and discipline are the main ties of a fighting unit, and if this tie is loosened then the unit is no longer of value."

"Then you tell us that this statement was not supposed to be obeyed, if the situation called for it?"

130

"I can only understand it so as I have just said it not, your Honor."

"Well now you have given us a lot of words but you haven't answered the question. Of your own volition you quoted this statement. The Court didn't quote it; it wasn't in the testimony theretofore. Now if you quote something you will either have to stand by it or repudiate it. The question is very specific. This statement which you have quoted is to the effect that in the German army it is understood that if the military situation—of whatever nature—calls for it, a soldier must shoot his own parents if he is ordered to do so. Now do you accept that statement or not? You have had enough time to give us an explanation. Now give us the answer. Do you accept this or you do not accept it as a fact? If the statement is meaningless, if it's just a lot of words thrown together without intention of impressing anyone with its veracity, then say so; but if it's intended to be obeyed, then say so."

"In my opinion this declaration was made in order to create an impression."

"But not to be obeyed literally?"

"That depends on the circumstances."

"Well, let us suppose a case where your superior officer tells you that the situation is such that the only way you can get out of it is for you to shoot your parents. Now that's an order. All right, now, are you going to live up to William the First or William the Second, or not?"

"In this situation it would have to be obeyed, your Honor."

"You would shoot your own parents if the situation required it."

"In so far I would have my psychological reaction, and I do not know whether based on this psychological reaction I carry out the order which has to be obeyed or whether I subject myself to punishment."

131

"Now you must answer the question. If the military situation is such that the only way you can be saved, according to what your officer tells you, is to shoot your parents, will you shoot them or not?"

"I cannot answer such a question, your Honor, in such a short time. That is a psychological struggle that I am not in a position to say yes or no."

Gloomily the defendant looked out the window at the diminishing light of the dying afternoon. I asked him, "Would you be ready to answer it tomorrow morning?"

"I don't know, your Honor."

I turned to Dr. Gawlik: "We will give him until tomorrow morning to think it over. The Tribunal will be in recess until tomorrow morning at nine thirty." As the defendants tramped out of the courtroom, and the judges retired to their chambers, the courtroom and corridors burst into a gallery of opinions. Spectators, lawyers, and court officers buzzed with predictions, speculations and guesses as to what Seibert would say on the following morning. Would he be better off by hypothetically slaying his mother and father or by outrightly disgracing his lawyer?

The next morning every seat in the courtroom was taken and the overflow visitors lined the walls two or three deep. In hotel lobbies, restaurants, and wherever people gathered the evening before, the absorbing topic of conversation had been whether Seibert, a professed moral disciple of the Kaiser of old, would be loyal to his Kaiser of today. One could not tell from Seibert's expression, as he waited in the dock, his eyes ringed red and his features pale and drawn, as to whether the night's worried deliberation had solved his dilemma. When the marshal called his name, he started, as if from a trance, and then, almost like a somnambulist, slowly advanced to

132

the witness stand. Allowing him time to gain his bearing, I repeated the question of the previous day: "Now, if in accordance with this declaration by the Chief of State of the German Empire at the time, the military situation made it necessary for you, after receiving an order to that effect from a superior officer, to shoot your own parents, would you do so?"

He blinked his puffy eyes as if to prolong his deliberations and then scanned the courtroom. Not once, however, did he look toward his fellow-defendants who obviously were on tenterhooks of anxious anticipation, more so than the spectators. Then, taking a deep breath, he expelled the words like one who had been hit in the chest: "Mr. President, I would not do so."

The audience broke into excited whispering and agitated elbow-prodding. The defendants' dock heaved a collective, heavy grunt of disgust. After rapping with my gavel for order, I proceeded to put another question: "Suppose the order came down for you to shoot the parents of *someone else*, let us say, a Jew and his wife. . . . The only thing that is established is that they are Jews. . . . The children are standing by and they implore you not to shoot their parents. Would you shoot the parents?"

Seibert now looked at only one person, and his looks were malevolent ones. He riveted his eyes on his lawyer, who had thrust him into this impossible situation where he was now defending the Jews against whom he had vowed violent antagonism for life. He clutched at the edge of the witness box and gasped, "Your Honor, I would not shoot these parents."

And then, closing the interrogation, I summed up: "And, therefore, as a German officer, you now tell the Tribunal that if an order were submitted to you, coming down the line militarily, to execute two innocent parents only because they were Jews, you would refuse to obey that order."

He replied: "I answered your example affirmatively. I said 'Yes, I could not have obeyed.'"

Thus, what had begun as a demonstration of the slavish obedience a German soldier owes to his military superior ended in a declaration by the proclaimer of that doctrine that he would not only ignore the order of the supreme war lord to shoot his own parents, but he would disobey an order to shoot anybody else's parents. He thus concluded, under his own interpretation of German Military Law, that a soldier was not a fettered slave.

It is remarkable how many people believe that a soldier is compelled to do everything his superior officer orders. A very simple illustration will show to what absurd extreme such a theory could be carried. Under such a doctrine, a sergeant could order the corporal to shoot the lieutenant, the lieutenant could direct the sergeant to shoot the captain, the captain could command the lieutenant to shoot the colonel, and in each instance the executioner would be blameless.

If a soldier is required, without inquiry, protest, or complaint, to put into effect the most patently unjust order, his superior officer could order him to shoot himself, and the soldier would have to turn his gun on himself, or otherwise be shot for disobeying orders! But if a soldier can protest an order (and he certainly can) which demands that he take his own life, he can protest an order which requires him to kill, for instance, an obviously innocent, harmless child.

It is true that a soldier's first duty is to obey, but it is also rudimentary common sense that his obedience is not that of a mechanical man. He is a reasoning agent. The fact that he may not, without incurring substantial

134

unfavorable consequences, refuse to drill, salute, exercise, reconnoiter, or even go into battle, does not mean there is no limit to what can be expected of him. To begin with, the order requiring implicit obedience must be one dealing with a military subject. Thus, an officer may not order a soldier to steal for him, or murder for him. And what a superior officer may not legally demand of his subordinate, the subordinate is not required to perform.

General J. Lawton Collins, Chief of Staff of the United States Army at the time, excellently put the matter when he said, "Discipline in our army cannot be founded upon a mechanical and uninquiring subservience, but instead must have as its keynote a respect for the rights and responsibilities of the individual."

Where a soldier or officer inferior in rank is actually coerced into executing an illegal order he will be safe from prosecution. No court, by way of illustration, would punish a man who, with a loaded pistol at his head, is compelled to pull a lethal lever. Nor, indeed, was any military person prosecuted in Nuremberg for carrying out an order of whose illegal implications he was totally unaware. The trials, where the military was involved, were of officers who had every reason to know that what they were doing violated laws of war and humanity. No private in the ranks of the Einsatzgruppen stood trial in the Palace of Justice at Nuremberg.

The I.M.T., addressing itself to this subject, well said, "The true test, which is found in varying degree in the criminal law of most nations, is not the existence of the [superior] order, but whether moral choice was in fact possible."

Rebecca West, with acidulous wit, approved. "It is obvious that if an admiral were ordered by a demented

First Sea Lord to serve broiled babies in the officers' mess he ought to disobey."

Before Adolf Eichmann was taken from Argentina to Israel he said, in anticipation of having criminal charges brought against him, that he was only a subordinate and was, therefore, required to obey the orders of his superiors. His only superiors in the program of Jewish extermination were Himmler and Hitler. Whether he went along willingly with the Fuehrer-Order, or was coerced into carrying out executions, can be ascertained from the testimony given at Nuremberg by his former deputy, Dieter Wisliceny, who was asked, "Did he [Eichmann] say anything at that time as to the number of Jews that had been killed?"

Wisliceny replied, "Yes, he expressed this in a particularly cynical manner. He said he would leap laughing into the grave because the feeling that he had five million people on his conscience would be for him a source of extraordinary satisfaction."

CHAPTER NINE

DID THE DEFENDANTS KNOW THAT THE FUEHRER-ORDER WAS illegal, immoral, and contrary to international law as well as national law? If they did not, they could not be convicted of crime because no subordinate may be punished for committing an act of whose illegality he is ignorant. The reputed ignorance, however, must be real and not feigned. The sailor who voluntarily ships on a pirate craft may not be heard to answer that he did not know what was expected of him. If he is charged with robbing and sinking another vessel he may not expect acquittal on a plea of superior orders, since anyone who willingly joins a criminal organization is assumed to be aware of its unlawful program.

What SS man could say that he had been ignorant of the Nazi policy with regard to Jews? As early as February 24, 1920, the National Socialist Party announced in its twenty-five-point program, which never changed, its pointblank hostility to Jews in every field of individual and social endeavor. *Mein Kampf* was dedicated to the doctrine of Aryan superiority. *Der Stuermer* and other publications spread the verbal poison of race hatred.

137

Nazi leaders everywhere vilified the Jews, holding them up to public ridicule and contempt. In November, 1938, hoodlumism, SS inspired and organized, fell upon the Jews of Germany. Synagogues were destroyed, prominent Jews were arrested and imprisoned, and a collective fine of one billion marks was imposed.

Did the defendants not know of these things? Could they express surprise when, after this unbroken, ever-mounting program of destructive violence, plans were formulated for the "final solution of the Jewish problem?" Suppose that the Fuehrer-Order, instead of ordering the slaughter of Jews, called for the killing of all gray-eyed people. So long as the iris responded to those light rays in the spectrum which make up gray, the possessor of such eyes was destined upon evil days. Character, occupation and health would not influence; religion, politics or nationality would not alter; intention, resolution and desire could not change the predetermined doom. The farmer at his plow, the teacher at her desk, the doctor at the bedside, the preacher in his pulpit, the old woman at her knitting, the children playing in the yard, the infant at its mother's breast—all would be condemned to death if they studied the wondering world through telltale gray eyes.

Let us look in on a family whose members, because of that unfathomable selection of life's chemicals and inscrutable mixing in the mystic alembic of time, all have gray eyes. Suddenly comes a thunderous knocking and the door bursts open. Steel-helmeted troopers storm in and with automatic rifles and drawn pistols order the dismayed occupants into the street.

We hear the screams of the terrorized women and children, the loud protests of the men, and the wild tramping of the invaders' boots through the house. We see the overturning of furniture, the smashing into cupboards, attics, and wardrobes in the seeking out of the hidden, horrified Gray-Eyed. We witness the tearful farewells to home, the piling into the waiting truck of the pitiful family possessions, the bewildered mounting of the doomed Gray-Eyes. The truck rumbles forward, stops to pick up other Gray-Eyes and still more Gray-Eyes in the market square, at the corner store, in the parish church.

This is followed by the wild careening ride into the woods where additional Gray-Eyes are waiting chalk-faced and mute, staring at one another. We watch the unloading of the truck, and hear the guttural command to line up. Now the red-mouthed machine rifles are speaking their leaden sentences from left to right and right to left. The villagers are falling, some cut in two, others with blood flowing from their mouths and eyes, those gray-eyes, pleading for understanding, for an explanation as to why? Why? Others only wounded still fall into the deep ditches. The shooting party rides away, piteous hands uplift from the uncovered grave, we hear a moaning which, at times, decreases to a murmur, then mounts to a wail, then ceases entirely.

Of course, this is all fantastic and incredible, but no more fantastic and incredible than what happened ceaselessly in the world of the Einsatzgruppen. If one substitutes the word Jew for Gray-Eyed, the analogy is unassailable.

It is to be assumed that if the defendants had been suddenly ordered to kill the gray-eyed population they would have balked and found no difficulty in branding such an order illegal and immoral. If, however, ten years before, the Nazi Party program had denounced all gray-eyed people, and ever since then the defendants had listened to Hitler vituperating against the Gray-Eyes; if they had seen shops smashed and houses destroyed because Gray-Eyes had worked and lived there; if they had learned of Himmler's ordering all Gray-Eyes into concentration camps; and then had heard speeches wherein the mighty chieftains of the SS had declared that elimination of the Gray-Eyes would enure to the benefit and profit of the executants of the annihilating program—if this had happened could we be so certain that the defendants would not have carried out a Fuehrer-Order against all gray-eyed people? And in that event, would there not have been the same defense of superior orders?

But the fact that Hitler would have denounced the gray-eyed population and that the ensuing persecution would have continued for ten years would not have made the atrocities any more legal than the atrocities perpetrated against the Jews. Any orderly person who did not have a personal motivation to spur him and a personal advantage to be gained from such a persecution would acknowledge the illegality and the immorality of the barbarous oppression at once.

But it was contended by most of the defendants that it was different with the Jews because the Jews were bearers of Bolshevism, and as such they constituted a threat to the security of the German armies which were fighting Russia. Ohlendorf testified that "the representatives of this blood [Jewish] showed themselves especially suitable for this idea; therefore the carriers of this blood became especially suitable representatives of the Bolshevism." But there was no proof that Jewish arteries were particularly equipped to accommodate Bolshevik corpuscles. In Germany and other countries where the Jews were not charged with harboring Bolshevik ideas they were killed just the same.

The defendant SS-Colonel Werner Braune tried to sustain the theory of Jewish-Bolshevik amalgamation. How successful he was in this thesis can be gathered from his testimony. I asked him, "Did you believe that the vast majority of the Jews assisted the Bolshevist cause?" He replied that he was "convinced of that."

I suggested to him that if the vast majority of the Jews supported Bolshevism, this meant that some did not, and could he not have conducted investigations before executions in order to exclude from death those who did not support Bolshevism?

He said that he did not believe that such investigations would be possible "practically and technically."

"If you conclude that the vast majority were in favor of Bolshevism, it necessarily follows that only a small minority did not approve of Bolshevism, is that right?"

"Your Honor, a small minority; that might have been ten, twenty, thirty percent."

"Well, all right. Let's say thirty percent. Thirty percent did not approve of Bolshevism. It would not be unreasonable to come to that conclusion?"

He observed that "there were a number of people who never cared one way or another."

"Well, give us just roughly, the percentage of those who did approve of Bolshevism among the Jews and those who did not. You say the vast majority did, would you say that is seventy percent?"

"I cannot give you a percentage, your Honor."

"Well, let it remain the majority. The majority then did approve of Bolshevism?"

"I am convinced of that, yes."

"Well, then, the minority did not."

"There is something between pro and anti. Somebody can be convinced and fanatical and prepared to fight to the bitter end and somebody can approve, but say, 'I don't want to have anything to do with fighting,' and somebody can be indifferent. Somebody can doubt and not be sure and somebody can conscientiously oppose it."

"Well, let's group them together just for the purpose of discussion. The majority approved. Let us say that is sixty percent. That is not quite as strong as a vast majority, but it is a majority, sixty percent. That leaves forty percent who either did not approve or were indifferent. That would be a just way of dividing it, wouldn't it?"

"Whether that is right, your Honor, I cannot say, but I am prepared to follow an example."

"Very well, you say the vast majority—let's say sixty percent, to be on the safe side—did actually approve of Bolshevism. Then forty percent—we are speaking of Jews all the time—either did not approve or were absolutely indifferent one way or the other. Now, when it came to executing a group, if you had excluded forty percent from the execution order, would that have caused any great difficulty?"

"Your Honor, there was no choice for me. I was in a war under martial law. I had an order from the supreme commander to shoot all Jews for the reasons given to us and it was not possible for me except to obey this order in war under martial law."

"Well, let's suppose that you had a way of determining that forty percent were not active Communists, couldn't you have found a way not to execute them?"

"No, your Honor, I must say that this possibility did not exist."

But can we accept Braune's answer that "this possibility did not exist?" The Einsatz leaders ruled vast territories. No ancient Roman emperor had more absolute authority over life and death than did these men. If they really had not wanted to kill defenseless people, they

142

could, by a nod of the head, or a wave of the hand, have saved populations from annihilation. The sad reality is that the Einsatz leaders had no desire *not to* kill Jews. The Fuehrer-Order was welcomed because it imparted what they considered a color of legality to what they wished to do because of personal satisfactions and advantages accruing to them. The killing of all Jews demonstrated conclusively that the Bolshevism argument was a dishonest one; even according to Braune's calculations some of the Jews were not Bolshevists.

In fact, for Braune the killing of Jews was so much a matter of routine that, in making up his reports on persons executed, he only mentioned Jews parenthetically. Referring to a search for "Communists and other untrustworthy elements," he said that "it was possible during the period covered by this report, to apprehend and shoot, for instance alone in Simpferopol *besides Jews,* more than one hundred Communist NKWD agents and saboteurs." (Emphasis supplied.)

Braune was not unwilling to describe what he had done. Our courtroom was equipped with a large wall map of Europe and Asia, embracing the area in which the four Einsatzgruppen organizations operated. Braune obligingly and courteously pointed out on the map various scenes of his activities with the ease and detachment of a college professor lecturing to a class of students. He reflected the confidence of the well-educated man that he was. He had obtained his degree of Doctor of Juristic Science when he was only twenty-four, and at the age of thirty-two had gone into the Einsatzgruppen, where he displayed a high sense of ethics in conducting killings. He explained that he refused to use gas vans because he did not think them honorable. "In my opinion an execution by shooting is more honorable for both parties

143

than the killing by means of a gas truck. This is the reason why I refused to use the gas truck."

Arguing that what he did was proper, Braune still said that he had entertained some "inner misgivings" about shooting unresisting civilians. However, he presented no objective testimony to show that reluctance. If he was really acting under compulsion and deplored the killings, he would have wanted, whenever the opportunity presented itself, to save some hapless Jew, if for no other reason than to be enabled, later on, to give substance to his contention that he was morally opposed to the Fuehrer-Order. I wondered if, at any time, he had released "some defenseless woman or whimpering child of the Jewish faith, who was scheduled for execution?"

"Your Honor, I did not see any whimpering child. I said how hard it was for us, and for me, and my men, to have this order carried out . . ."

"You know that since children were killed, they certainly wouldn't go to their death laughing—since you seem to object to the phrase 'whimpering child.'"

He said that he did not object to the phrase, but that there were no exceptions. Later on, I returned to the subject, thinking that in the meantime he might have recalled an exception. "You did not, in complying with that order, attempt to salve your conscience by releasing one single individual human creature of the Jewish race —man, woman or child?"

He was as constant as a professor of geology. "Your Honor, I have already said that I did not search for children. I can only say the truth. There were no exceptions, and I did not see any possibility."

But the inevitable query recurs: Is this credible? Braune was separated from the bastions on the Rhine by mountains, lakes, rivers, forests, vast plains, countless

144

cities and millions of people. He would have encountered no difficulties in clandestinely taking a boy or girl by the hand and leading him or her away from the execution pits, if only that he might say in later years, in the event Hitler's boast for a thousand-year Reich should go awry, that he did have "inner misgivings" about the Fuehrer-Order, and that on one occasion he did save a dirty-faced, whimpering child.

But, like Adolf Eichmann himself, Braune had no interest in saving Jewish children. In his memoirs, Eichmann describes attending an Einsatz execution near Minsk where five thousand Jews were put to death:

"When I rode out the next morning, they had already started, so I could see only the finish. Although I was wearing a leather coat which reached almost to my ankles, it was very cold. I watched the last group of Jews undress, down to their shirts. They walked the last 100 or 200 yards—they were not driven—then they jumped into the pit . . . Then the men of the squad banged away into the pit with their rifles and machine pistols.

"Why did that scene linger so long in my memory? Perhaps because I had children myself. And there were children in that pit. I saw a woman hold a child of a year or two into the air, pleading. At that moment all I wanted to say was, 'Don't shoot, hand over the child . . .'"*

But Eichmann did not say, "Don't shoot, hand over the child." He remained mute and the child was shot.

Though Braune on occasion said he had felt some "inner misgivings" about the Fuehrer-Order and the massacres he conducted under its aegis, he never made any effort to be relieved of his assignment. Since he was under Ohlendorf's immediate command and admitted that he was on friendly terms with Ohlendorf, I sug-

* Life Magazine, Issue November 28, 1960.

145

gested he might have said to Ohlendorf, "It is very difficult for me to execute this order. Can't you do something
to save me from it? Can't you put me on some other
assignment?"

Braune frowned at the idea. "I believe Herr Ohlendorf
would have considered me a shirker if I had done this
and he would not have had the slightest understanding in
spite of our good relation."

"Well, then, you were more afraid of being considered
a coward than to take the chance in asking him to relieve
you from this task which you found so onerous and dis-
tasteful?"

"No, your Honor. I was convinced that there would be
no point in it, and that Herr Ohlendorf would not have
been able to do anything."

In point of fact, Braune did not need to subject himself to the opprobrium of either being called a "shirker"
or of being part of a conscience-shaking project, since
Ohlendorf had testified, "In two and a half years I had
sufficient occasion to see how many of my Gruppe did
not agree to this order in their inner opinion. Thus, I
forbade the participation in these executions on the part
of some of these men, and I sent some back to Germany."

The jewel of consistency which glittered as Colonel
Braune held it aloft did not lose any of its luster or gleam
as it passed into the hands of SS-Lieutenant Colonel
Adolph Ott, another defendant, who, when he was asked
if he had ever released a Jew, replied, "I believe in such
matters there is only one thing, namely, consistency,
Either I must shoot them all whom I capture or I have
to release them all."

In February, 1942, Ott took over the command of
Sonderkommando 7b in Einsatzgruppe B at Bryansk, on

146

the Desna River, some 220 miles from Moscow, and remained in that area, upholding the integrity of the Fuehrer-Order, until January, 1943, during which period he conducted from eighty to one hundred executions. In justifying these killings he said that the subjects of the executions deserved death since they were either partisans or saboteurs. He knew this to be true because he questioned them before he shot them. I inquired what he did if it developed that a Jewish prisoner had not committed any crime. Was he shot?

He seemed surprised at the question. Why, of course, he was shot, he replied.

Pausing a moment to get over my astonishment, I put the obvious follow-up query: "What was the necessity of the investigation if the result was that he always would be shot? What was the reason for wasting all this time on a man you were going to shoot anyway?"

But Ott was not as much a spendthrift of time as might at first seem apparent. He interrogated his prisoners in order to obtain information which could lead to the apprehension and execution of others!

But what if a prisoner refused to give information about others? He was shot just the same.

"Some of them refused to talk?"

"That is so."

"And they were shot just the same?"

"They had to be shot if they were Jews."

The real truth was now emerging. "Well, then, you did shoot some Jews because they were Jews?"

"I have already said, your Honor, every Jew who was apprehended had to be shot. Never mind whether he was a perpetrator or not."

Ott was even more specific. "I told my Sub-Kommando leaders that Jews after they are seized and do not belong

147

to a partisan movement or sabotage organization must be shot on the basis of the Fuehrer-Order."

However, it must not be assumed that Ott was wholly inconsiderate of prisoners. He related: "In June 1942, without having received an order to do so, I opened an internment camp in Orel. In my opinion people ought not to be shot right away for comparatively small misdeeds. For this reason I put them in this internment camp, in which the people had to work. I determined the length of time that these people should remain in the camp on the basis of examination and investigations of the individual cases which were made by my kommando. It happened too that people were released."

Ott's magnanimity in this concession was probably even greater than he intended to express. His nobility of soul manifested itself not in the fact that he said "people ought not to be shot right away for comparatively small misdeeds," but in his assertion that it "happened too," that is, it *even* happened that some people were not shot!

Whether one who executes an order acts willingly or under compulsion can best be determined by the manner in which he proceeds to put it into effect. The defendant SS-Lieutenant Colonel Eduard Strauch could hardly have been accused of lacking sympathy for the Fuehrer-Order.

Strauch was an interesting figure. On the day of the arraignment he provided drama for the audience and exciting copy for newspapermen. As Judge Dixon asked him, "Eduard Strauch, are you represented by counsel before this Tribunal?" he uttered a shriek and toppled to the floor in an epileptic seizure. He was taken out by court attendants. It apparently occurred to him later that he could use this temporary or periodic incapacitation as evidence of insanity. A medical board, however, examined him and reported "that the defendant, Eduard Strauch, except for brief periods preceding, during, and succeeding epileptic seizures, is capable of understanding the proceedings against him and of taking adequate part in the direction and presentation of his defense."

The resourcefulness which prompted him to feign mental unbalance had its prototype in the ingenuity which enabled him to devise clever methods whereby his Einsatzkommando 2 of Einsatzgruppe A could kill over fifty thousand Jews in a matter of several months. So as to avoid the possibility of opposition from, or rioting among, his victims, he would loudly announce to the truck drivers, whose vehicles were filled with Jews, that they were to drive to varying destinations, thus conveying the impression to the passengers that they were to be taken to different places for resettlement. Previously, however, Strauch would have instructed the drivers to proceed to a single rendezvous—the mortuary ditch in the woods.

Anyone who so put his heart into his work could scarcely honestly say that he disliked it. One day he even invaded the office of his superior, the General Commissioner of White Ruthenia, seized seventy Jews and spirited them away for prompt execution. A grim commentary on this piece of business lies in the fact that Strauch almost got into trouble over it. The General Commissioner complained to headquarters, not because Strauch had killed seventy innocent human beings but because a subordinate had dared to come into his office and shoot "his" Jews *without telling him* about it!

Strauch said that whatever he did, he did for the "cause." Thus he resented the fact that there should have been criticism because, before the Jews were shot, he had their dental gold fillings removed. "I emphasized," he growled, "that I could not understand how German men could quarrel because of a few Jews. I was again and again faced with the fact that my men and I were reproached for barbarism and sadism, whereas I did nothing but my duty. Even the fact that expert physicians had removed in a proper way the gold fillings from the teeth of Jews who were designated for special treatment had been made the topic of conversation." The charge of sadism against this SS-chief could hardly be dismissed lightly. Two scars which slashed across the left cheek of his skull's face like stiletto tracings accentuated the sinister aspects of this born killer.

It would happen at an occasional execution that a brave prisoner would spit at his executioners as he was being led to his waiting grave. It was quite enjoyable then for a man like Strauch to spit back with a submachine gun, the fire bursting forth from a muzzle which never turned on its operator. What a satisfaction for the killer then to see the spitter falling headlong into a hole. And then the piling of the earth; the inordinate contentment of burying Hitler's enemy. This was victory, this was triumph, this is what the Fuehrer asked for—called for in his speeches urging the SS, the glorious SS, on to greater victories and greater glories. Imbued with this kind of septic frenzy it was natural that Strauch would voice the observation that consideration for the Jews was "softness and humanitarian daydreaming," and that it was unthinkable that a German should listen to Mendelssohn's music; and that to hearken to Offenbach's *Tales of Hoffman* revealed a woeful ignorance of National Socialistic ideals. In his attitude toward music composed by Jews, Strauch may have been inspired by an incident in the life of Adolf Eichmann who, when only a private in the SS, beat up two Bavarians for playing

150

Jewish phonograph records. This vigorous display of anti-Semitic aggressiveness, which came to the attention of his superiors, helped Eichmann in his climb up the SS ladder.

When Strauch, with a palpably exaggerated dragging of feet, first propelled his way to the witness stand, he responded to the questions with irrelevant answers and volunteered statements which gave clear evidence, even to a medically untrained ear, of an ordered disorder and a patterned absence of pattern, all undoubtedly aimed at achieving an adjudication of mental, and therefore, criminal irresponsibility. But one day he became so absorbed in the narrative of his exploits that he completely forgot his pose. His eyes gleamed with the remembered glory of his past Einsatz days and with obvious self-satisfaction he told of sixty to ninety executions he had personally attended, and recalled watching woman and children lining up to be shot. Then, with a quick calculation, he stated that as nearly as he could remember the number of persons he had killed totaled seventeen thousand.

CHAPTER TEN

NEXT TO OHLENDORF, PAUL BLOBEL WAS PERHAPS THE defendant who excited the most notice among the visitors, who numbered not only Nuremberg residents but travelers from all parts of the world. Nuremberg from late 1945 to 1948 was a Mecca to historians, writers, dramatists, journalists and diplomats who recognized in the proceedings unfolding in the Palace of Justice the serious attempt being made to establish international responsibility to law by individuals, as well as nations. While Ohlendorf arrested attention because of his good looks, Blobel drew awed glances for the opposite reason. As he sat in the front row in the defendants' dock his square red beard jutted out ahead like the prow of a piratical ship commanded by himself. His eyes glared with the penetrating intensity of a wild animal at bay. It was hard to believe that this ferocious-looking creature was once an architect handling weapons no more lethal than a sliding rule and colored pencils.

The Einsatzgruppen reports showed that Sonderkommando 4A, which Blobel commanded from January, 1941 to June, 1942, killed over sixty thousand persons. His attorney, Dr. Willi Heim, was indignant over these reports and claimed they were not accurate. The truth of the matter was, he said, that Blobel could not have been responsible for the killing of more than fifteen thousand!

As Blobel strode from the defendants' dock to the witness stand, he seemed to change in aspect from a villain of the sea to a mountaineer guerilla chieftain. Encased in a large military jacket with four enormous flapped pockets and numerous buttons, which somehow suggested bandoleers bulging with cartridges, he fired his answers as if from an automatic rifle. His whole expression shouted that it was absurd he should be charged with crime. He was fighting a war; the reports were wrong; he did not kill as many people as they charged him with. Moreover, all cases were investigated before executions took place. And then he asserted that he committed no crime since his shootings were authorized by international law.

When Prosecutor Horlik-Hochwald asked him: "Did you not have any moral scruples about carrying out executions—that is, did you regard the carrying out of these executions as in agreement with international law and in agreement with humanitarian impulses?" his beard bristled with the resentment of one who has just listened to a preposterous as well as insulting question.

Why, the executions of "agents, partisans, saboteurs, suspicious people, indulging in espionage and sabotage, and those who were of a detrimental effect to the German Army," he stridently rejoined, "were, in my opinion, completely in accordance with the Hague Convention."

He did not stop to name any article of the Convention which authorized the killing of "suspicious people." Nor did he manifest the slightest awareness of the terrible reality that killing on mere suspicion is the very essence of first degree murder. Othello will wash for many an eon in "steep-down gulfs of liquid fire" before he will be cleansed of the guilt of strangling Desdemona.

When his attorney asked him if he had any moral scruples against the execution of women and children, Blobel replied that he did not, because "every spy and saboteur knew what he had to expect when he was arrested." He did not specify in what manner women and children were spies and saboteurs.

Another explanation he offered for executions was that they were in the nature of reprisals. He believed that the killing of ten of the enemy for one German soldier "murdered" was not disproportionate because "other countries also carried out reprisal measures, and have given orders for such reprisals, about one to two hundred according to the well-known order of General Eisenhower."

Surprised to hear this statement, I asked, "You say there is a well known order of General Eisenhower that two hundred were to be executed to one?"

Testily he replied, "All the German people know, your Honor, that an order was given by General Eisenhower that for every one American who was killed, two hundred Germans are to be shot." The defendant had become a prosecutor.

The courtroom was filled with people, many of them obviously German. I swept my hand from left to right to encompass the entire audience. "In this courtroom there must be, undoubtedly, many Germans. Can you point out one who knew of this order which you have just stated?"

The bearded accuser sat rigidly in his chair and made no answer. I inquired of Blobel's attorney if he knew of such an order. Bowing low, his robe scraping the floor, Dr. Heim said, "No, your Honor."

I asked the defendant whether he had personal knowledge of the order, and when he said that he had not read it himself, I inquired if any attorney in the courtroom knew about the order. To this question, he answered in the affirmative. I directed my glance at the score of lawyers sitting at the defense tables and at the several lawyers at the prosecution table. "Does any attorney here know about the order, yes or no?"

Blobel shot out, "Yes."

"Which one?"

"Dr. Heim, for example, read about it."

"Dr. Heim has already denied knowing about any such order. Mention the next person."

"I don't know the other gentlemen as well. I said I presume that people knew it."

He suggested that perhaps Ohlendorf was acquainted with the order, but Ohlendorf was now allowing himself one of his rare smiles. He hated Blobel because he regarded him as a liar and enjoyed seeing him, as he told others later, "stewing in his own juice."

To my question as to whether he could point to one defendant "who can state that he saw this announcement," Blobel replied, "I'd have to ask each one individually."

I faced the dock: "The Tribunal will direct a question to all of the defendants. The witness has stated—of course, you have heard what he just stated—that an order was issued by General Eisenhower that for every Allied soldier killed, two hundred Germans would be killed . . . Did any of the defendants here in this court ever see such an announcement? If any one did, he will please raise his hand."

Passing up Ohlendorf, Blobel turned the fiercely burning candle power of his eyes on the defendants, one after another, seeking by sheer ocular strength to lift one hand out of the two score available to confirm his utterance. But not a finger lifted or turned. The whole defendants' dock had turned to stone. I waited for a minute or two and then addressed the glowering Blobel: "No defendant has raised his hand, so now we come back to your original statement, that all of Germany knew of this announcement. Do you want to withdraw that statement?"

The bold and haughty beard had drooped to its owner's chest. The flaunting mustache had also wilted. Through the whiskery jungle came a mumble: "Under those circumstances, I have to beg your pardon."

Blobel was the evil genius of the notorious Kiev massacre. Sometime in September, 1941, the Jews of that city were instructed to appear in the public square on the 29th of that month with all their belongings, since they were to be "resettled." They responded in multitudes, eager to rid themselves of a city bewildered and reeling under the battering fist of war. A long procession of trucks rolled up to haul them to the "resettlement" area, where they were immediately taken before the execution rifles. Never had Blobel as an architect planned and executed a building project so efficiently as he did this razing of human lives. The victims were spared long delays, the anguish of doubt, the inconveniences of lack of shelter and food, and worry as to what might happen to their property and valuables.

So expertly did the ex-builder organize the truck service, the firing squads, and the burial teams that at the end of the second day 33,771 persons had been killed and entombed. And in the meantime every item of the "resettled" people's property had been gathered and catalogued, not only with governmental survey proficiency, but with the supreme virtue of charity dominating all. The official report stated that "Money, valuables, under-

156

wear and clothing were secured and placed partly at the disposal of the USV (Nazi Party Public Welfare Organization) for use of the racial Germans, partly given to the city administration for use of the needy population."

But with his charitable instincts gratified, Blobel was still not entirely content, for the report informs us further: "The Jews who were not yet apprehended as well as those who gradually returned from their flight again to the city were in each case treated accordingly."

In Zhitomir, some eighty-five miles from Kiev, and then on his return to Kiev, Blobel continued his intensive drive in behalf of charity. The clothes taken from his victims in these latter operations required the service of numerous auto-cars. A report dated November 12, 1941, announced that "137 trucks full of clothes, made available in connection with the campaign against Jews at Zhitomir and Kiev, were put at the disposal of the NSV."

Blobel willingly described just how he conducted executions. He related how he divided his extermination unit into shooting squads of thirty men each, after the long ditches had been dug. "Out of the total number of the persons designated for the execution, fifteen men were led in each case to the brink of the mass grave where they had to kneel down, their faces turned toward the grave. When the men were ready for the execution one of my leaders who was in charge of this execution squad gave the order to shoot. Since they were kneeling on the brink of the mass grave, the victims fell, as a rule, at once into the mass grave.

"I have always used rather large execution squads, since I declined to use men who were specialists for shots in the neck (Genickschusspezialisten). Each squad shot for about one hour and was then replaced. The persons which still had to be shot were assembled near the place

157

of the execution, and were guarded by members of those squads, which at that moment did not take part in the executions."

I must confess that I did not easily adjust to the contemplation of this vast and calloused extermination of human life, but finally came the time when I could ask questions on the frightful details of executions without a hesitant voice or any visible emotion. And so I asked Blobel if he attached any type of marker or sign to the victims in order to guide the aim of the riflemen. If my voice was firm, Blobel's was as steady as a howitzer as he replied that the men of his unit were expert shots.

Nevertheless, I had misgivings, so I went on. "Striking a vital spot in the body requires a very steady hand, a very good eye and perfect control of the nervous system. Would you say that all these riflemen were so well-trained that they could bring home their shot to a vital spot in the victim's body at all times?"

An audible shudder ran through the spectators in the courtroom for they could visualize as well as I the possibility that a person only slightly wounded could be buried alive. But Blobel said that this was impossible. "After each firing order, when the shots were addressed, somebody looked at the victims, because the victims were then put into the grave when they did not fall into the graves themselves, and these tasks were in the field of tasks of the men of the individual kommandos. The edge of the grave had to be cleaned, for instance. Two men who had spades dealt with this. They had to clean it up and then the next group was led there."

I still worried about the possibility of a conscious person seeing the coffin lid of earth closing over him. "Since this was all done rapidly, might it not be possible that a victim would be buried, even though not actually dead?"

"No, that is quite impossible, your Honor."

158

"You exclude that possibility?"

"Yes, for the simple reason that if it was ascertained that the shots which had been aimed at the head had not actually hit the head, one of the men of the firing squad was called in, who fired again [with rifle] from a distance of three to four paces. He shot again and thus it was made absolutely certain that the person concerned was dead."

A slight noise at the foot of the bench caused me to look down. The girl court reporter, who was recording the testimony, held a convulsive hand to her mouth, smothering a gasp, while the other moved over her notebook. Perhaps she pictured, as I did, the blood-curdling scene of the headhunter bearing down on his helpless, frozen-eyed prey, and firing at three paces.

Although Blobel asserted that he acted legally at all times, he was concerned about the evidence he left of his executions. He flew back to Berlin and called on his chief Adolf Eichmann in his office at Kurfstenstrasse 116. From him he obtained an order authorizing the opening of graves and burning of corpses. The burning process, however, was not as satisfactory as Blobel had hoped, so he resorted to other means. He tried dynamiting. Rudolf Hoess, commandant of the Auschwitz concentration camp, who supervised this operation, stated that this evidence-destroying method did not measure up to expectations. "Blobel constructed several experimental ovens and used wood and gasoline as fuel. He tried to destroy the corpses by means of dynamiting them, too; this method was rather unsuccessful." Hence other means were used:

The ashes, ground to dust in a bone mill, were thrown in the vast forests around. Staf. Blobel had the order to locate all mass graves in the entire Eastern territory and

159

to eliminate them . . . The work itself was carried out by Jewish work units, which, upon finishing their particular task, were shot. Concentration camp Auschwitz had to furnish continuously Jews for this kommando.

Despite these attempts to dissolve the ghosts which could rise to haunt him, Blobel was boastful of his bloody handiwork. A witness, Albert Hartel, testified regarding his association with Blobel in Kiev in the month of March, 1942. One day Hartel drove into the country accompanied by Blobel who called his attention to various points of interest. Suddenly Hartel was frightened by a terrestrial phenomenon—the earth was exploding. Under the questioning of Dr. Heim, Blobel's own lawyer, as to additional information, Hartel said, "I cannot give any further details of this drive because it made a shattering impression on me at the time. It was snowy, and on one particular spot we touched the spot, the earth still exploded. There were some kind of eruptions, a kind of explosion, and I asked Blobel what that was, and he said, 'Here my Jews are buried.'"

Blobel knew his worth. When Prosecutor Horlik-Hochwald, reading aloud from a document which contained Blobel's name, asked him if his name was Paul Blobel, the bearded and mustached dignitary stood up as well as he could while still sitting down, and declared, "My name is Hermann Wilhelm Paul Blobel."

Eichmann, who on occasion stood by Blobel's side as he gave the order to fire, regarded him as one of his most effective executioners in the occupied territories. Accordingly he would from time to time invite him to Berlin to deliver lectures before his Gestapo staff of specialists. In one lecture, delivered in November, 1942, Blobel graphically described the methods he employed in opening graves and cremating bodies of executed Jews.

160

It is easy to understand, after a panoramic view of this necromantic titan's bouts with blood and graves, why the defendant Eugen Steimle, who served in the Einsatzgruppe with Blobel, in commenting on personages he had known in that organization, summed up Blobel as "Bloodhound, brutal, without inhibitions, unpopular."

If there ever was an understatement worthy of recording, it is that last word.

Regardless of their mode of procedure, the executioners commended themselves on the magnanimous methods they observed in accomplishing their missions. Defendant after defendant emphasized to the Tribunal that the requirements of militariness and humaneness were fastidiously complied with in all killing parties. Of course, occasionally, as Otto Ohlendorf described it, "the manner in which the executions were carried out caused excitement and disobedience among the victims, so that the Kommandos were forced to restore order by means of violence," that is to say, the victims were beaten.

The defendant SS-Brigadier General Erwin Schulz also assured us that "useless tortures" were avoided.

How did the people destined to die react to their fate once they became aware of its irrevocable finality? According to the defendant Paul Blobel, most of them were silent. Some of the prisoners, who were to be shot in the back, turned around at that last moment and bravely faced the riflemen, but still they said nothing. The executioners could not understand this muteness—but what did they expect these piteous mortals to say? What words could be found to speak to this unspeakable assault on humanity, this monstrous violence upon the dignity of life and being? The helpless doomed were silent. There was nothing for them to say.

161

When Blobel commented rather disparagingly on this silence, I asked him, "You mean they resigned themselves easily to what was awaiting them?"

He replied: "Yes, that was the case. That was the case with these people. Human life was not as valuable as it was with us. They did not care so much. They did not know their own human value."

I winced at this self-satisfied and grim comparison of life values.

"In other words, they went to their death quite happily?"

"I would not say that they were happy. They knew what was going to happen to them. Of course, they were told what was going to happen to them, and they were resigned to their fate, and that is the strange thing about these people in the East."

"And did that make the job easier for you, the fact that they did not resist?"

"In any case the guards never met any resistance or, at least, not in Sokal. Everything went very quietly. It took time, of course, and I must say that our men who took part in these executions suffered more from nervous exhaustion than those who had to be shot."

"In other words, your pity was more for the men who had to shoot than for the victims?"

"Our men had to be cared for."

... "And you felt very sorry for them?"

"Yes, these people (the riflemen) experienced a lot psychologically."

CHAPTER ELEVEN

NATTY SS-BRIGADIER GENERAL ERICH NAUMANN AFFECTED a short, bright tan military jacket in the courtroom. With regular features and an excellent military bearing, he must have struck an impressive figure as, arrayed in general's uniform, with gleaming boots and a shining sword, he led his columns to the execution grounds, all to the glory of Adolf Hitler and the purification of the Aryan world.

From Smolensk, Russia, he had sent Eichmann the reports before us. One of them related that during the month of November, 1941, his Einsatzgruppe B had conducted executions in sixteen different areas, resulting in the killing of 17,256 Jews, men and women—as well as the slaying of sixteen children in a children's home. Another report spoke of executions between March 6th and 30th, 1942, numbering thousands of persons. Although some of the deaths in this report were labeled as punishment for "theft," "attempted murder," "sabotage" and "spying," most of them were listed simply under the designation of "Jews," "gypsies," or "membership in the Communist Party." Naumann acknowledged that his Einsatzgruppe possessed two or three gas vans which "were used to exterminate human beings."

Like Braune and Ott, Naumann subscribed to the "no exception" rule. When I asked him if he thought that "in order to win the war it was necessary to kill hundreds of thousands of defenseless people, men, women and children, unarmed," he replied unhesitantly in the affirmative.

Later, however, he probably felt that he had committed himself too far and withdrew to the sheltering statement that he did entertain some misgivings about the Fuehrer-Order. I now naturally assumed that he was conceding it was wrong to kill blameless populations, especially women and children, and accordingly asked him if that was so. But he replied, as a wave of surprise rippled through the courtroom, "Not wrong, your Honor, because I was given the authority to do so, because there was a Fuehrer decree."

However, still later, his answers again began to drift toward a definite acknowledgment of evil in the Fuehrer-Order, and I consequently put the question: "Therefore, you thought there was something wrong about it, something morally wrong?" But, again, unexpectedly, he replied, "No."

"You saw nothing wrong in mowing down these defenseless men and these helpless women and children? You saw nothing morally wrong in that?"

"Not unjust, your Honor."

Since there was no doubt about Naumann's participation in the killings attributed to him and his unit, the only question left for us to resolve was whether he shot down the thousands listed in the reports because he wholeheartedly approved of the Fuehrer-Order, in which event his guilt would be established conclusively, or whether

164

he was compelled, against his will, to conduct executions, in which case the verdict would favor him. Thus, it was vital to the decision of the Tribunal that we know if Naumann perceived any illegality in the Fuehrer-Order. To a question directed toward getting an answer on this specific point, he replied, "Your Honor, I know that my yes or no will be very decisive and I do not hesitate to answer."

But he did hesitate, and in the heavy silence which followed I sought to relieve the tension by explaining that all we wanted was the truth. He either thought the order was right or it was wrong. Which was it? "There is certainly no disposition to coerce you to give one answer or the other." I pointed out the extraordinariness of the fact that under the Fuehrer-Order people were shot down without opportunity to defend themselves or even to protest. "Now you either agreed with this order or you did not agree with it."

His voice vibrant, he replied, "Yes, your Honor, I did agree with it."

But as soon as these words left him, he seemed to regret having uttered them. He looked fixedly ahead as if realizing that here at Nuremberg he was standing at the crossroads of world reckoning. The muscles of his throat visually tightened as I assumed he was preparing to say that his conscience had bothered him and that he did entertain qualms about executing an order whose savage scope might have shocked the feelings of even a cannibal king. But still he wavered. He apparently could not bring himself to repudiate the man who had made him a general with the greatest power that can be bestowed on any mortal, that of issuing unappealable decrees of death. He withdrew to the ramparts of his original decision that he approved of the Fuehrer-Order.

165

Wanting to make certain that this was his well-considered conclusion, I asked, "And then you had no reluctance about putting it into effect because you agreed with it?"

His fingers played a tattoo on the ledge of the witness box; he blinked several times. A sense of moral guilt was now perhaps suggesting an answer which would show to the world that he was not without honor. "I already said that I had misgivings. It was with reluctance and it was a fight between duty and conscience and the realization that this measure was necessary in order to fight Bolshevism."

I was, of course, aware, as he had himself said, that his answers could be decisive. Accordingly, I wanted him to take all the time he needed in which to reflect fully on what he had done and how he would account for what he had done. "Then you did not agree with the Fuehrer-Order completely? Let me point out to you, witness, that when a soldier goes into battle, he has no misgivings. He is going in to fight. He knows that his opponent is armed. He knows that he is fighting for his country and he may kill. Further, afterwards, if he comes out alive, he goes home and he sleeps tranquilly at night; he has no misgivings, no regrets. On the contrary he may be enthusiastic over the combat he waged. But here you say you did have some misgivings; you did entertain some reluctance, so, therefore—" and here I paused, while the whole world seemed to pause with me. The defendant sat as still and quiet as the bronze hourglass attached to the wall. Equally the whole courtroom settled into the stillness of statuary. Sunlight streaming through the windows cast on the floor distorted shadows of the human tableau; it fell on the witness chair and brightened Naumann's military jacket until it shone like burnished armor. Time seemed to stop.

166

Clearing my throat to complete my statement, I started at my own voice: "So therefore, I ask you whether or not you did not believe at the time that there was something wrong with the order."

Again there was silence. Outwardly Naumann was as still as the bronze hourglass, but inwardly, undoubtedly, the pendulum of deliberation pitched in alternating decision. Which did he prefer: To stand high in the estimation of his Fuehrer, even though he was dead? Or to seek the respect of the world, thousands of whose guiltless inhabitants he had slaughtered? He turned slightly in the chair so that he could face me directly. He straightened out the wrinkles in his jacket, and in a modified, respectful voice he answered, "No, your Honor, I considered the decree to be right, because it was part of our aim of the war and therefore it was necessary."

So that there could be no doubt about his decision, I pointed out the interpretation we could take from his words. "Then the Tribunal will accept from your answer that you saw nothing wrong with the order, even though it did involve the killing of defenseless human beings. That is what we draw from your answer."

He nodded in affirmation: "Yes, your Honor." And as he stalked back to the prisoners' enclosure, one could almost imagine his doing it to the Wagnerian strains of *Götterdämerung*.

The attitude of SS-Colonel Walter Blume was a little different from that of General Naumann. He said that he obeyed the Fuehrer-Order because he was compelled to do so although actually it filled him with revulsion. However, despite this supposed revulsion, he told us he urged upon his men the reasonableness of the order. With a scar which began at the left corner of his mouth and extended halfway across his cheek, it seemed, as he

167

testified, that his speaking outlet had had to be enlarged by surgical operation so that he could make speeches to his Sonderkommando 7A which did its part in wiping out what one of his reports declared to be "racially completely inferior elements."

It was not difficult to visualize Blume, with his slanting forehead and elongated mouth, as he stood before his men ordering them to load and cock their rifles and then stentorianly addressing them in the following language, which he repeated in Court: "As such it is no job for German men and soldiers to shoot defenseless people, but the Fuehrer has ordered these shootings because he is convinced that these men otherwise would shoot at us as partisans or would shoot at our comrades and our women and children were also to be protected if we undertake this execution."

Blume also explained from the witness stand: "This we would have to remember when we carried out this order." But he did not remember to say that the men, women, and children he ordered killed had not committed any crime or shot at anybody. He only remembered that the Fuehrer had said these people "would shoot" at them, their women and children—a thousand and more miles away. In other words, the Jews were to be killed because of the *possibility* they might at an unknown time in the unknown future be of some danger to the Fuehrer and the executioners. Blume said he made this speech to ease the feelings of his men, but what he was really doing was convincing them how proper and justifiable it was to kill innocent and helpless human creatures. If he had actually believed the order to be unjust, conscience would at least have restrained him from falsely defending it on the basis of justice and reasonableness. His exhortations probably persuaded his men into the en-

168

thusiastic accomplishment of other executions which might otherwise have been avoided entirely or less completely fulfilled.

Evidently foreseeing that the proposition might be put to him that if he regarded the Fuehrer-Order as unjust he could have avoided it by simply sending in a false report, he volunteered a refutation to the unspoken charge. "A false report did not occur to me. I would have considered it unworthy of myself." And then he added as an afterthought, "Apart from this my personal attitude about giving a false report, it would have been discovered very soon and it would have brought the same results as an open refusal to obey, namely, my sentence to death."

Of course, if the latter alternative were the more probable of realization, there would be, on the basis of self-preservation, justification for Blume's refusal to misreport. However, since he offered two contradictory excuses I asked which of the two motivated him to kill rather than to falsify. He replied:

"Your Honor, today I cannot exactly put myself in a situation, which one of these two thoughts dominated at the time, but they were both very close and both faced me barring a way out."

I insisted on an answer. "But those two reasons can't be reconciled. It is like a person who must decide whether to steal a hundred dollars or not and a conflict arises in his mind: 'If I steal this money I am being dishonest and I would not be true to myself; it is not correct, it is not moral—that is one reason. And then, for the second reason, I may get caught and they might send me to jail.' But here the second reason completely nullified the first because in the latter case he was not debating the problem morally; he was concerned only with the fear that he might "be caught."

Blume seemed offended with the illustration. He squared his shoulders; he was a man—and he declared with emphasis that "the feeling that a false report was unworthy of me induced me not to take such a way out."

Thus, he found it more manly to kill people he knew to be without fault than to tell a lie to his superiors in Berlin—several civilizations away.

This presents an interesting subject for reflection. The man who must choose between honor with sacrifice and dishonor without sacrifice would prefer naturally not to be forced into choosing between such alternatives. But no one can be assured, in the complexities of life, that he will not be required to make momentous decisions. Blume had the choice between the physical fact of murder and the abstract concept of equivocation. He had to decide which was more honorable: to write up a report stating that five hundred men, women, and children had been killed although they still lived, or to take these helpless human creatures out into the woods, shoot them down pitilessly and fling them into graves with the possibility that some of them might still be alive.

One defendant stated that to have disobeyed orders would have meant a betrayal of his people. Did he really mean that the German people, had they known, would have approved of this unrestrained butchery? The masses of the home-loving German people, more content to have a little garden in which to grow a plant or two than a promise of vast lands beyond the horizon, now got to learn, through the Nuremberg trials, how they were betrayed by their supposed champions. How much inhumanity, how much oppression, how much of innocent blood has been shed throughout history in the name of

170

the "People," whose only desire is to be allowed to live at peace with their neighbor, unharassed by restless, ambitious and greedy chieftains so determined to lead them to riches and glory—over a precipice.

Blume was very solicitous about the health of his men. After a spell of executions he would take them out into the country by the shores of a beautiful lake where they found diversion and recreation. He testified, "They were particularly grateful for this. We started every day with sports. In the evenings I had songs sung at the campfire."

But there were no songs sung in the thousands of homes he had emptied of father, mother and babies. For Blume, there was only one home and that was his own, to which he expected to return, crowned with laurel wreaths he would place at the feet of the man to whom he had entrusted his conscience and who represented for him the law of the world. When Blume spoke of an incident where he had executed three men because they had urged some farmers not to bring in a harvest for the Nazi invaders, Mr. Ferencz asked, "Are you familiar with the rules of war?"

"In this case I acted by carrying out the Fuehrer-Order which decreed that saboteurs and functionaries were to be shot."

"Did you regard a person who told a farmer not to assist the Nazi invaders as a saboteur—only because he refused to help the Nazis—as worthy of the death sentence which you invoked?"

"Yes."

"Are you familiar with the rules of war?"

"I already stated that for me the directive was the Fuehrer-Order. That was my war law."

Blume stated that he "admired," "adored," and "worshipped" Hitler because what Hitler did was right. His

171

ideas of what constituted right may be gathered from some of his answers regarding Hitler's invasion of neutral countries.

"You believe that it was proper to make war on Norway, which had not declared war on Germany?"

"Your Honor, I can only repeat that at the time it was explained to us quite clearly and we believed this."

"You believed it was proper?"

"Because we believed . . . We would be first this way."

"Well, regardless of what was told you, you believed it was proper to invade Norway?"

"Only because of what I was told."

"You believed it to be proper in view of what had been told you?"

"Yes."

"And you believed it was proper to invade Denmark and Holland and Luxembourg?"

"All this was connected with the statement that we had to carry out this in order to avoid that they attack us."

"Well, you believe that it was proper?"

"From that point of view, yes."

"You believed it was proper to invade Greece?"

"At the time there were differences already."

"But you believed it was proper. That is the only thing I want to find out."

"Yes, your Honor."

"You believe it was proper to invade Yugoslavia and Belgium?"

"Yes, we were told at the time."

"Now, do you justify all those invasions today? Do you think today that it was proper to have invaded all these countries?"

"Your Honor, I have no possibility to study history here."

172

"Do you believe today it was proper to invade Norway, Denmark, Holland, Belgium, Luxembourg and the other countries?"

"I can't reply to this, your Honor."

Blume felt that Adolf Hitler "had a great mission for the German people." It did not matter to him what this mission might mean to the rest of mankind. With all other members of the Nazi Party he voluntarily took the Fuehrer-oath: *I vow inviolable fidelity to Adolf Hitler; I vow absolute obedience to him and to the leaders he designates for me.* By this absolute submission of his will to that of Hitler, Blume completely scuttled the defense of superior orders. When anyone willingly abdicates all independent thinking and tenders himself as putty into the hands of another, he cannot complain if he is punished for the crimes plotted and planned by the other with whom he stands inviolably in agreement. For let it be said once and forever that Hitler with all his cunning and unmitigated evil would have remained as innocuous as a rambling crank if he did not have the Blumes, the Blobels, the Braunes and the Bibersteins to do his bidding—to mention only the B's.

CHAPTER TWELVE

LOOKING INTO THE DEFENDANTS' DOCK, ONE SAW EDUCATED men, but he would have difficulty in determining, from facial features and expressions alone, which was the most learned of all. It is not likely, therefore, that the one who in fact had had the greatest volume of academic instruction would be the one selected, on appearance, as the Nestor of the group. Professor Franz Six, by some strange process, seemed to have become less intellectual-looking with each scholarly distinction conferred upon him. Six was a graduate of the University of Heidelberg where he specialized in sociology and political science, becoming a Doctor of Philosophy in 1934. In 1936 he received the high academic degree of Dr. phil. habil. from the University of Heidelberg, and became Dozent in the faculty of law and political science at Koenigsberg; later, he passed examinations for the Venia Legendi at the University of Leipzig. By 1938, he was Professor at the University of Koenigsberg, and by 1939 he had obtained the chair for Foreign Political Science at the University of Berlin and was its first Dean of the faculty for Foreign Countries. In spite of all this, he still looked more

174

bibulous than bibliophile. His exaggerated slouch seemed to emphasize the disorder of his rumpled suit and to suggest a snobbish glint to the glasses perched not too certainly on his nose.

Armed with the formidable scholastic ladder above indicated, Six quickly climbed to the rank of Brigadier General in the SS organization, which he joined early in life. When Einsatzgruppe B was formed, he was placed at the head of Vorkommando Moscow which, of course, was committed to the Fuehrer-Order as were all other units in the Einsatzgruppen organization.

But Professor Six indignantly denied from the witness stand that he had anything to do with killing Jews, even though reports showed his unit carrying out the Fuehrer-Order. He said that his principal function with the Vorkommando was to collect documents and archives, but engaging in such a collection did not exclude participation in executions. Hitler had ordered the liquidation of all political functionaries. The lists of such persons were to be found among the "documents and archives" that Six collected which, when obtained, were turned over to the firing squads.

Six maintained that his interest in Jews was purely scientific. The nature of this scientific interest can be gathered from a speech made by him in April, 1944, in Krummhuebel at a session of consultants on the Jewish question, an excerpt from which read, "The physical elimination of Eastern Jewry would deprive Jewry of its biological reserves. . . . The Jewish question must be solved not only in Germany but also internationally."

In spite of this exhortation to Semitic annihilation, Six testified that he was a very tolerant man. Settling back in the witness chair with the air of a man whose education is too broad and profound to permit of the littleness

175

of racial prejudice, he explained why it was impossible for him to be an anti-Semite. Why, two of his very best teachers, when he was working on his doctor's thesis, were Jews. He said that he not only had great respect for those two Jews but regarded them as friends. He had often visited them at their homes and even after he had left the university he had corresponded with one of them. I asked him what was his attitude toward these two Jews when the Nazi storm of violence broke over their heads. He shrugged his heavy shoulders: "I regarded it in any case as highly unpleasant that these people were concerned in new laws and regulations."

But he thought that the Jews had really not suffered greatly. When it was suggested to him that millions of Jews had been persecuted, he jerked his head forward in quizzical challenge. "What do you mean by persecution?"

His question was answered. "Now, Professor Six, a man who has been a dean of a university and a professor and a journalist and a newspaper man and a general and a soldier—with all of your experience, for you to ask what is meant by persecution seems a little trifling. You know it means from personal insult up to deliberate killings. Now, that is what is meant by persecution. It ran the whole gamut from the simplest kind of an insult to the last solemn crime of killing defenseless people and burying them in unmarked graves. That is the definition of persecution. Did you feel offended when all the Jews were persecuted?"

After this explanation, he said that he thought it was a "shame and a scandal" that Jewish synagogues should have been destroyed by fire, but he detected nothing improper about the executions performed under the Fuehrer-Order.

176

Like David taking Goliath's measure, the short Benjamin Ferencz looked up at the tall Six and, with scorn
edging his voice, asked, "You stated when you learned of
the burning of the synagogues, as a German it struck you
as a shame and a scandal. I am asking you as a German
did it strike you as a shame and a scandal when you
learned of the murder of defenseless people?"

Six shook off the question with the equivocating "it
depends on circumstances."

But Ferencz was not to be shaken off. He insisted on a
definite reply, Six demurred, Ferencz repeated the question, Six was annoyed, but finally his big pedagogic brain
swung into action: "The fact that synagogues actually
burned and that no steps were taken to prevent this, I
regarded as a shame, as a German and as a human being;
but I cannot regard an order as a shame. It is, after all,
the contents of an order, but not the order itself. I cannot say that an order is a scandal. If the Chief of State
issues an order, I can only regard it as a human being,
and I am prepared to regard and to judge it as a human
being, but I cannot say that an order is a scandal, an
order by the Chief of State."

With this answer, Six stripped away his own veneer of
education and culture and stood revealed in all his primitive prejudices. Although years had passed since the
Fuehrer-Order was promulgated; although the whole
world stood aghast at the crimes laid at Hitler's door;
although Germany lay in rack and ruin as the result of
Hitler's absolutism; although Six and his co-defendants
were charged with offenses which could merit the death
sentence—in spite of all this, he still refused to acknowledge that Hitler's order to kill innocent Jews was "a
shame and a scandal."

His answer so astounded me that I felt the need of a

confirmation. Accordingly I asked him if he did not consider the execution of Jews also "a shame and a scandal."

He replied: "Must I answer this question?"

I said: "If you don't want to answer, the Tribunal will have to assume that you don't want to make a comparison between the destruction of an inanimate conglomeration of stone, brick, and mortar, and pulsing live human beings. You are indicted and you voluntarily take the stand. No defendant is compelled to take the stand if he does not wish to, but once he takes the stand, he is subject to cross-examination and then, if he volunteers statements, certainly those statements are open to inquiry."

Mr. Ferencz now put the question again: "When you learned of the execution of Jews as a result of the Hitler Order, did you regard it as a shame and a scandal?"

This time Six was willing to concede that it was a shame and a scandal "if defenseless women and children are concerned," but he would not go the whole way and admit the same about defenseless men because the killing of the defenseless men, he said, was "the expression of the Fuehrer-Order."

A great German scholar, Wilhelm von Humboldt, who founded the University of Berlin where Six had been professor and dean, defined, as far back as 1809, "the limits beyond which the activities of the State must not go." But for Six there was no such limitation. At Hitler's behest he had lowered the wick in the lamp of his learning, and thus he could see nothing wrong in the world, even massacre, so long as Hitler directed it. Six's great faith in his leader did not go unrewarded. He was promoted "for outstanding service in Einsatz" by the most learned professor in the history of the human race on the subject of murder—none other than Heinrich Himmler.

178

SS-Colonel Martin Sandberger also believed that the Fuehrer-Order was legal since Hitler was the "supreme and unrestricted legislator." Sandberger commanded Sonderkommando 1A of Einsatzgruppe A in Esthonia and also served as commander of Security Police and SD in that country for a total of twenty-six months. During that period synagogues were destroyed, Jews were executed and pogroms were incited, but Sandberger denied that he ever committed an illegality. The most he did was to imprison Jews for their own security, he said. What happened to them after imprisonment can be gathered from a report dated October 15, 1941: "At present a camp is being constructed in Harku in which all Esthonian Jews are to be assembled, so that Esthonia will be free of Jews in a short while."

Round-faced and juvenile-looking (he was thirty-six years of age) Sandberger conveyed the impression of someone telling tall stories at a crowded bar. Nor did the tales he related dissipate that impression. He testified, for instance, that he never permitted an execution which had not been preceded by investigation and trial. He said he established a court system of inquiry, appeal, review, and re-review which involved three different courts, made up of twelve persons, including himself.

If there had been the slightest semblance of a trial for the persons executed under his orders, it would not have been difficult to present evidence to support the assertion. The Nuremberg defense lawyers were given the utmost freedom to gather evidence in any country, clime, or habitat, but not one witness appeared, not one document was presented, to support Sandberger's story. Apart from the lack of evidence to substantiate his assertion, it would be absurd to expect that there could have been so elaborate a court procedure to protect the very people scheduled for summary extermination under the precise order which gave Sandberger authority to act at all.

He told us of one case where he ordered eight hundred to nine hundred Jews into an internment camp in Esthonia. Since internment was usually the first step toward execution I asked him if he investigated before ordering internments. His answers illustrate rather graphically Sandberger's ideas about investigations.

"Did you investigate the cases of any of these eight hundred to nine hundred Jews?"

"Yes."

"How many?"

"I cannot give you the number."

"Why can't you give us the number? . . ."

"I cannot remember this figure."

"Well, was it five hundred?"

"If I must give an estimate, it may be about eighty to one hundred."

"Why didn't you examine the other eight hundred, or seven hundred? Do you think it was fair to examine only eighty to one hundred and not examine the rest? Is that your idea of justice?"

Sandberger was a lawyer. He was trained to think fast. He said he had two reasons why he did not examine all the internees. "One reason is that Stahlecker had urgently ordered a general internment, and I could not evade this." (He never told us the second reason.)

"Why did you evade it for the eighty to one hundred you did examine?"

"There the investigations took place because in connection with other cases which were investigated, namely Esthonian Communists, with whom these Jewish cases were connected; and, therefore, interrogations had to take place."

180

This was fast thinking but he did not look ahead far enough.

"Did you examine these eighty yourself?"

"I personally took no investigations myself."

On another occasion Sandberger said that in Pskov he herded four hundred and fifty Jews into a concentration camp for their own protection, feeling quite confident, he remarked, that the Fuehrer-Order would soon be revoked. The Jews later fell before firing squads. Sandberger explained that this was not his fault. The execution occurred without his knowledge and while he was away.

This explanation was reduced to shreds under Prosecutor John Glancey's raking cross-examination fire.

"You collected these men in the camps?"

"Yes, I gave the order."

"You knew that at some future time they could expect nothing but death?"

"I was hoping that Hitler would withdrawn the order or change it."

"You knew that the probability, bordering on certainty, was that they would be shot after being collected?"

"I knew that there was the possibility, yes."

"In fact, almost a certainty; isn't that right?"

"It was probable."

There was another occasion when he was absent and more Jews were shot. Again he pleaded ignorance but he did not caution the executioner not to do it again.

"In this conversation which you had with him, did you or did you not say to him, 'I don't want you to do this again.'?"

"No, I didn't tell him."

Sandberger's "work" was not hidden beneath the

181

bushel of unappreciation. The citation recommending him for promotion for his "assignment in the East" proclaimed that "he is distinguished by his great industry and better than average intensity in his work."

SS-Brigadier General Erwin Schulz could have been a bank vice president chosen to persuade wealthy depositors into making large investments in the bank's business. Dignified of demeanor, gray-haired and urbane, courteous in speech and manner, he seemed misplaced in the dock sitting between the martial-looking General Naumann and the self-satisfied Professor Six. He was apparently just as courteous and considerate on the execution grounds commanding Einsatzkommando 5 in Einsatzgruppe C, because he performed his executions, he said, "in a serious and dignified manner." He was the officer, as previously stated, who insisted there be no "useless torture." He divided his Kommando into three platoons. "The first platoon was placed face to face with the persons about to be executed, and about three men each aimed at each person to be shot." With a keen sense of delicacy, General Schulz would avert his head as the rifles were aimed. Then, after the volley had been fired, he would turn around and see that "all persons were lying on the ground."

Schulz said that he was trained in the art of nobility because he taught the subject of chivalry at school.

He said that he never killed Jews simply because they were Jews. Admitting that he did kill Jews in an action at Lemberg, Poland, he explained that that action was in the nature of a reprisal because, before his arrival there, five thousand persons had been killed by "Jewish officials and inhabitants." He said that "participants and suspected persons were arrested and that an order from

182

Hitler required that "guilty persons or even stongly suspected persons be shot."

In summing up the case against Schulz at the end of the trial, Deputy Chief Counsel James M. McHaney, devastated Schulz's argument that the Lemberg action was a reprisal action. "Schulz must have known, and undoubtedly knew, that the German occupation forces had no right or reason for the carrying out of reprisals for the killing of Poles and Ukrainians which had taken place before this occupation. These Poles and Ukrainians who were the alleged victims of the Communists and Jews of Lemberg were not members of the German Armed Forces. They were not citizens of a country allied to Germany; on the contrary, they were nationals of countries which had been attacked by Germany in breach of international treaties and in disregard of International Law . . ."

It is thus quite evident that the Jews killed at Lemberg were killed only because they were Jews.

Like Sandberger, Schulz sought to escape responsibility for some of the killings charged against him by asserting he was not present. But if the executions were ordered before he left the scene of operation, his absence at the time of the actual firing did not absolve him. The terrorist who sets the clock on a time bomb, conceals it in the cellar of his victim's house, and then departs, is most assuredly absent when the explosion occurs, but his guilt is as absolute as that of the assassin who plunges the dagger.

Schulz's attorney saw in his client a man with a "liberal" attitude toward Jews. Of course, he added, that it went "without saying that he wanted to reduce again the tremendous influence of Jewry in his fatherland to normal proportions."

183

It was this "spirit of reduction" which headed the columns of the relentless Einsatz killers as they pursued their bloody way through the Ukraine, the Crimea and other distant parts of the world, reducing helpless men, women and children to dust and the human spirit of the slayers into something that can only make one ashamed that the human race could produce anything so vile.

The defendant SS-Colonel Eugen Steimle was not to be outdone by Sandberger in the matter of punctilious observation of the code of civilized peoples in conducting trials and investigations before executions. Tall, long-faced, and lugubrious-looking, Steimle told the Court about his "examinations." He testified that among those he executed, following examinations, were "active Communists." In order to obtain a concrete illustration of what he meant by "active Communists" I asked him what he would do if he entered a room and found someone advocating Communism to a group of five to ten people. I specified that this speaker was in no way opposing the Germans; only expatiating on the theories of Karl Marx. Would Steimle order such a person shot? Steimle replied, "I would have got a look at the man, and if I was under the impression that he would put his theoretical conviction into deed, in that case I would have had him shot. The actual speech or lecture could not be decided upon theoretically."

I repeated the hypothetical situation. "So that you would listen to the speech and then you would look at him under a microscope, and after this big look, if you thought he might have done something, then you would have him shot. That is what we understand by your answer?"

And to this he answered with a categorical "Yes."

184

Steimle commanded Sonkerkommando 7A of Einsatz-gruppe B from September, 1941 to February, 1942, operating in Western Russia between the river Dnieper and the Volga. He admitted that his Kommando carried out between one hundred and one hundred and fifty executions but said that the people executed were partisans, "persons suspected of being partisans," and Russian soldiers who "disregarded our order to give themselves up." He said that Nebe, who was chief of Einsatzgruppe B, had complained that Steimle's Kommando when "fighting Jews so far had not been shooting women and children," and insisted that they had to be "shot likewise."

But Steimle refused to shoot women without a trial or an investigation, he said. And in this connection he told of three girls he had arrested—one a school teacher, another a school inspector; he did not remember the occupation of the third. He related that he seized these girls because "they were about to form a partisan group." He assured us that he investigated the case and then shot the girls. Whether any investigation actually occurred could only depend on Steimle's testimony. He gave no details as to the method of investigation so that it would seem that his inquiry as to whether the girls "were about" to form a partisan group was no more extensive than the one he gave in the hypothetical case as to how he would determine who was an "active Communist." He admitted that he personally commanded the firing squad which ended the lives of the three girls, and assured the Court that he saw to it that "three or four men shot at one woman."

Steimle's whole attitude with regard to executions can probably be gathered from replies he made to questions put to him by Chief Prosecutor Ferencz: "Approximately how many people would you say were killed in September in Velikki Luki?"

"That I cannot say. I have no idea."

"Was it more than one hundred? Was it less than one hundred?"

"I don't know."

Finally, almost jadedly, he said, "I think it must have been less than one hundred."

"Well, you say now that you know that in September you shot people in Velikki Luki and you have no idea of how many people it was. You just remember shooting people."

"I was only in Velikki Luki once or at the most twice."

It was perhaps rather unfair of Mr. Ferencz to expect a man whose business was killing to recall just how many people he had slain in Velikki Luki when he had been there only once or twice. It would be like asking a shoe salesman how many shoes he sold in Oshkosh during a certain month when he had been there but once or twice.

CHAPTER THIRTEEN

DEFENDANT SS-LIEUTENANT COLONEL WALTER HAENSCH obviously decided that his best defense was a denial of everything. The cynic who said, "If they catch you with your knife in your victim's heart, deny, deny, deny," could not have had much to teach Haensch. The Einsatz records showed that on January 16, 1942, Haensch arrived in Artemowsk, Russia to take over the command of Sonderkommando 4a. A report of that Kommando announced that on March 6, 1942, it killed 1224 Jews. Confronted with this report, Haensch denied that he was responsible for the killings because he didn't really arrive in Artemowsk until March 15, 1942. What delayed him? He said that he was held up in Berlin for a dental appointment, a session with a photographer, and a farewell party. It is contrary to all military traditions that in wartime an officer's assignment to an important task could be delayed two months for the trivial reasons related by Haensch. Was Haensch telling the truth?

Lantern-jawed and wearing thick glasses, he seemed to be standing behind an impenetrable mask as he insisted he knew nothing about the massacre. He went further and said he had no knowledge of the execution of Jews under the Fuehrer-Order. He even maintained that his predecessor in command of Sonderkommando 4A never once mentioned the subject of Jews to him. The predecessor was none other than SS-Colonel Werner Braune who at no time manifested any particular reluctance in talking about Jews—or in shooting them. Was Haensch telling the truth when he said that the Jew-killing Braune was utterly silent about the matter which was engaging his whole enthusiastic and undivided attention?

"He did not mention Jews at all?"

"No."

"Did the word 'Jew' ever fall from his lips in his conversations with you?"

"Your Honor, I don't know now but I can't imagine, the idea of measures against Jews . . ."

". . . Did the word 'Jew' ever fall from the lips of Werner Braune when he discussed with you what were your duties as his successor?"

"I don't know, your Honor. I cannot remember."

"Did it or did it not?"

"No. I can't remember."

After taxing the credulity of all hearers on the subject of his conversation with Braune, Haensch sought to stretch the tissue of gullibility even further. Although, according to his own calculation, he arrived only a few days after the massacre of the 1224 Jews, he said that not a member of the Sonderkommando which performed the butchery ever mentioned the subject once.

"Now, assuming that you were not there when this happened . . . don't you think that at some time or another something would have been said about the execution of these Jews by the very men that you had now taken over in your command?"

"No, your Honor."

I felt that on a matter of this importance the Tribunal should not be satisfied with a mere negative response, so I continued the examination: "You have now stated that you have no reason to doubt the correctness of these reports. Therefore, if 1224 Jews were shot by your organization before you took over, does it not seem strange to you that in all the time that you were with the very men who conducted the execution, not a word was ever said about so extraordinary a phenomenon as the execution of 1224 human beings simply because they were Jews?"

Haensch was obviously determined not to be led into an admission, regardless of incongruity. "Your Honor, I can only say, I did not know anything or hear anything about this at the time. In particular I did not know the Fuehrer-Order until the moment here in Nuremberg."

This startling statement that he did not know of the Fuehrer-Order until he was brought to Nuremberg for trial, at least four years after the order had become the byword of every Nazi official, and every SS officer and enlisted man, was so palpably a fabrication that I could not abandon the interrogation.

I reminded him that he admitted the correctness of the reports and then asked him for the third time how he could explain the fact that although 1224 people had been killed by his organization just before he arrived, nothing was ever said about it to him. "Does that not seem strange to you?"

Though the guns of incredulity might explode in his face, Haensch stuck by them. "Well, your Honor, nothing was mentioned and nothing was said about it."

But Haensch was not so ignorant of executions as he tried to make it appear. Prior to the trial he had written out in his own hand a twenty-five-page statement on his Einsatz services, over eight pages of which were devoted

189

to a discussion of executions and his manner of conducting them. ". . . I was requested to make statements concerning the number of executions, which in my estimation were carried out by the Kommando according to orders during my time as leader of the Sonderkommando 4B. To this I must state the following: In the absence of records I am no longer able to give such information. An estimated number would lack any basis of fact. For this reason and those reasons as stated above, I cannot give such an estimate."

Haensch's inability even to *estimate* the number of executions performed by his Kommando while he was its chief is practically conclusive, if words have any meaning, that the number was not a small one. There is additional reason for this conclusion. His long, eight-page description of executions reveals a familiarity with mass killings which no one would associate with dilettantism in the matter. Let us look at several sentences taken from his volunteered statement:

> The executions were effected by shooting from the nearest sure-aim distance. That distance, as I recall it, was not more than 8-10 paces.
>
> . . . .
>
> I must once again energetically repudiate the assumption that the shootings were carried out in a mean manner, e.g., in the form of mass shootings by machine gun bursts from a considerable distance or by shooting in the neck or in an otherwise low-down manner.
>
> . . . .
>
> I myself watched a few executions. Where possible this was done in a manner so as to surprise the execution command by my sudden appearance.
>
> . . . .
>
> I still remember that the absolutely necessary insuring of instantaneous death without previous mere wounding

190

was brought up during those discussions, and that it was emphasized to aim at the head as a sure guarantee for instantaneous death.

Haensch said that he never executed a person without first affording him a trial. He said also that he reviewed the evidence in cases where the army ordered him to perform executions. It developed, however, under cross-examination by Prosecutor Horlik-Hochwald, that Haensch would review cases without any written report on what had happened.

"If you didn't receive a written record outlining the offense committed by the person that you were now to execute, how did you know what was his offense, and how could you review the evidence to determine whether it justified an execution?"

"The facts of the penalty for the crime committed by them were named to the subcommander by the military person ordered to carry it out."

Thus Haensch made no review at all. But how much, in any case, could Haensch be believed? He said that when Streckenbach announced the Fuehrer-Order in Pretsch, he failed to discuss the very enterprise to which he committed Haensch; that Heydrich, who delivered lectures on the objectives of the Einsatzgruppen, was silent about killing Jews; and that Thomas, the actual chief of Einsatzgruppe C, under whom Haensch operated, remained mute on the specific topic of the Gruppe's principal function. One would have to have the most credulous ears that were ever attached to the human skull to accept these disclaimers as true, but Haensch went beyond fantasy when he said that the first time he ever heard of the Fuehrer-Order was when he arrived in Nuremberg for trial!

191

The short and frail-appearing SS-Brigadier General Heinz Jost, who commanded Einsatzgruppe A in Esthonia, Latvia, Lithuania and White Ruthenia, was not so crude in his denials of guilt. He did not ask us to believe that he never heard of the Fuehrer-Order to kill Jews. He only asked us to believe that he did not *remember* ordering any Jews to be shot.

"Do you recall ever having received a report that Jews were killed by units under your command?"

"At the moment I cannot remember that. Certainly I do not remember any reports about mass executions during my time."

Jost was not devoid of natural intelligence and he was by no means uneducated. He studied at the Universities of Giessen and Munich, majored in law and economics, and held office in the District Court in Darmstadt until he became active in Nazi politics. In addition to becoming a Brigadier General in the SS, he attained the high rank of Major General of Police. Could a person with the mental equipment this record indicates, even though calloused to carnage and mass killings, dismiss from his memory the sea of blood over which he moved to his headquarters?

Jost arrived at the encampment of Einsatzgruppe A on the Gulf of Riga on March 29, 1942. Prior to this date the Gruppe had killed one hundred thousand people and as late as March 26 the volleys of its action squads were still echoing through the Gruppe's headquarters. There was no reason for the Einsatzgruppe, only three days before Jost's arrival, suddenly to stack arms, with the Fuehrer-Order still in full effect. If the firing ceased, it must have been only to give the riflemen a rest while the gas vans took over.

It was also while the defendant Strauch was under the

192

command of Jost that he executed fifty-five thousand Jews. Even if Jost had been as forgetful as Professor Six he could not possibly have forgotten fifty-five thousand murders!

SS-Lieutenant Colonel Gustav Nosske was another absent-minded defendant. He could not remember how many persons he had killed, even though I strove mightily to prod his memory. "We do not ask you to give us a precise figure and then hold you to that figure. That isn't the purpose of the Tribunal at all. We know that memory is a fallible function of the brain, but we also know that memory cannot discard the recollection of horrible events. Now the killing of a human being is the sum total of horror. It is the ultimate in human distress, and whether you are on the receiving end or the giving end of death, it makes its imprint on the brain and on the heart in such a way that nothing can eradicate it. So when we ask you to recall how many people you ordered executed, we don't expect you to give one definite precise, unchangeable figure, and then, if that should vary from another figure, say that it would appear you had purposely lied. We do, however, expect that you can, as a reasonable and rational person, offer some judgment, some estimate on this very serious business of killing people."

But despite his profound study of economics, banking, and law, Nosske could not recall just how many people had fallen before his firing teams. He could, however, remember, he said, that it was fortunately his lot never to have to kill Jews only because they were Jews. Could this story be believed? He said he was summoned to Berlin and there given command of one of the first detachments assembled to kill Jews in the East. He set out with motor vehicles, machine guns, sub-machine guns,

193

rifles, carbines and pistols, and took his Kommando directly into a territory heavily populated with Jews— but neither he nor his unit ever fired a bullet at a Jew. But how did he put in the time? Oh, he helped the Russian farmers bring in their wheat; he assigned his men to assisting ethnic Germans; and then on occasion they reconnoitered for partisans.

Jauntily attired in a sports jacket and wearing a butterfly bow tie, Nosske had no trouble in meeting his lawyer's questions—he was answering from a prepared script. However, when questions from the prosecution attorneys and from the bench did not fall within the scope of his anticipated interrogation, he revealed the true state of his feelings regarding Jews. Since he said he had not encountered any Jews in Russia I asked him what he would have done if, armed with the Fuehrer-Order, he had come across five hundred Jews. Would he have killed them? Without any equivocating he replied that if his Einsatzgruppe chief would have been in a position to "reprimand" him for disobedience, he probably would have killed them.

Later on, he said that if he had been placed in such a situation he would have conferred with his conscience, which prompted the question as to what he would have done after conferring with his conscience.

"Now, you are before five hundred innocent people, men, women and children—Jews—and you are presented with this order to kill them. Now, are you going to confer with your conscience and, if so, what is going to be your conclusion?"

"I would have taken it upon my conscience."

"And you would have killed them?"

"I would have probably done it."

But Nosske's activities in mass killings were not re-

194

stricted to hypothetical adventures. There were moments on the witness stand when, being carried away by glittering memories of Einsatzgruppen he punctuated his testimony with reiterated references to shootings and executions, *e.g.*: "From the twenty-first of June until the fifteenth of September certainly, because during the time from the tenth to twenty-fifth or twenty-third [of August], the shooting in Babtschinzy took place and then later on several shootings took place . . . This territory where the Kommando XII moved was declared Romanian sovereign territory; certain shootings occurred but we didn't quite know. Our own and other people's reports mentioned this . . . Of course shootings were carried out, in particular in this whole territory, and shootings were reported about on the principle that not only our own shootings but also shootings by others were reported later on including events which had been in other territories."

Eventually shooting apparently became so hackneyed an operation for Nosske that there was an occasion when he refused to shoot a certain assemblage of Jews—not out of charity or sympathy but because it meant just that much more work for him. He related how, one day, while following the course of the Dnestr River north of Romania, he came across an encampment of from seven thousand to eight thousand Jews at a place called Jampol. He made inquiries as to what they were doing there and learned that they had been driven from their home in Mogilev which was on the other side of the river.

Prosecutor Walton asked him, "Now, do you know why these Jews were expelled from their homeland by the Romanians?"

Lackadaisically Nosske replied, "I have no idea. I assume that the Romanians wanted to get rid of them and sent them into the German territory so that we would have to shoot them, and we would have the trouble of shooting them. We didn't want to do that. We didn't want to do the work for the Romanians, and we never did, nor at all other places where something similar happened. We refused it and, therefore, we sent them back."

CHAPTER FOURTEEN

WHILE MANY OF THE DEFENDANTS CANDIDLY ADMITTED their participation in the executions reported by the organizations they commanded, it was to be expected that some would deny such complicity. In those cases cross-examination, which is the X-Ray machine searching for fractures in the bones of truth, played an important part in determining credibility. And we now come to the case of SS-Lieutenant Colonel Ernst Biberstein, who, as an executioner, was in a class by himself. He was a ex-clergyman.

While most of the defendants had not forbidding personalities, two of them really looked as they would be expected to look in a Hollywood representation of their characters. These men were Ernst Biberstein and Paul Blobel, who could vie with one another for honors in inelegance. In such an unsavory contest Biberstein would probably win because he had traveled further than Blobel in the transformation from educated decency to unrestrained depravity. In court he wore a black shirt which throughout the trial gave no evidence of much laundering. His suit hung on him like a rag bag.

Biberstein was ordained a minister in the Lutheran

Presbyterian Church and held a pastorship in Schleswig-Holstein from 1924 to 1927, succeeeded by a similar post in Kaltenkurchen until 1933. He then became presiding minister of the Provincial Protestant Church in Bad Segelberg, Holstein. While so engaged in the house of the Lord, he saw nothing unseemly about slipping out the back door to participate in Nazi meetings where the prevailing doctrine differed from what he was presumed to be preaching in the pulpit. Later, he joined the Nazi party as a full-fledged member, and in 1938 he formally separated himself from the church. However, before he took off his clergyman's robe, he joined the SS. He then went the whole way and accepted office in the dreaded Gestapo which regarded the concentration camp as an ideal substitute for the church, and *Mein Kampf* as an improvement over the Ten Commandments.

In September, 1942, at Rostow, on the Don River, he took charge of Sonderkommando 6, Einsatzgruppe C. Prior to becoming a Kommando leader he had shown an intense interest in a plan headed by Eichmann to solve the "Jewish problem" by shipping all Jews to Madagascar. Before Eichmann could get this "resettlement" plan in operation, however, Hitler decided to attack Russia and the Einsatzgruppen came into being. This pleased Biberstein very much. With an extermination unit at his disposal he saw no reason for transporting the Jews to Madagascar, with all the expense such an enterprise would involve. Why not solve the problem directly? He answered his own question. In a sworn statement made prior to the trial he stated that from September, 1942, to January, 1943, his Kommando killed from two thousand to three thousand people. At the trial he challenged the correctness of his own figures but refused to name any other figures.

198

Prosecutor Horlik-Hochwald thought that I allowed Biberstein too wide a latitude in presenting his defense. But, considering the gravity of the charges and, if convicted, the gravity of the penalty this ex-minister of the gospel faced, I felt I could not open the doors of defense evidence too wide. Thus, in addition to allowing him maximum scope in introducing evidence in his behalf, I ruled that the prosecuton should exhibit to him, if he desired to see it, all documentary evidence that had been gathered in his case. Mr. Horlik-Hochwald protested: "I don't know the International Military Tribunal ever ruled that the prosecution has to submit documents which are in favor of the defense."

I ruled, "If the International Military Tribunal did not so declare, this Tribunal will declare that whatever the prosecution has which is favorable to the defense must be submitted."

"If your Honor please, I don't want to challenge this statement. I only wanted to explain here that the International Military Tribunal ruled, nothing else. I did not want——"

"Well, if the International Military Tribunal said that, this Tribunal overrules the International Military Tribunal, because it is not in accordance with the principles of justice that either side may withhold anything which may shed light on the issues before the court."

Biberstein took full advantage of the privileges accorded him. Having seen the prosecution's evidence which outlined the territory in which he operated, which was an area covering sixty thousand square kilometers, including several large cities, he said that although he traveled throughout that region with his Kommando, he not only did not kill Jews; he never even saw a Jew! He also professed complete ignorance of the Fuehrer-Order and said

199

that the leader of his Einsatzgruppe and his comrades not once even talked about Jews.

"In all your conversations with him [the Einsatzgruppe leader] he never mentioned that Jews were to be killed?"

"No. My conversation always dealt with certain subjects."

"And he never mentioned Jews."

"No, we never talked about this kind of tasks, as I already explained."

"And your brother Kommando leaders—they never talked about Jews?"

"Well, we never had any reason to do this. I only met other Kommando leaders who were leaders in Perpape-trowsla and in Stalino where I spent the night on my way from Kiev to Rostov."

"And in your conversations with them nothing was ever said about killing Jews?"

"I never talked to these men about their tasks and their activities because I was inexperienced in that and I did not like to show any inexperience constantly."

"And they never mentioned Jews?"

"No, we talked about quite different subjects."

In view of Biberstein's history, these statements overshot the sphere of belief, but it was not enough merely to assume incredibility. A witness's believability has to be tested. Since it is the responsibility of a presiding judge, by continental standards of court procedure, as already stated, to ascertain the facts, and to delve into motivations behind certain answers in order to get at the truth, I felt the need to question Biberstein for the purpose of determing on what scale of reliability his answers could be weighed. He had said that when he commanded the Gestapo in Oppeln, he did not order a single person into a concentration camp. I asked him if he had ever recommended the commitment of anyone to a concentration camp. He replied that he did not remember.

"Well, would you say definitely that you did not?"

"As far as I know, I never did that. I would have remembered now."

"Well, you put it in a negative fashion. You say you don't remember. That includes the possibility that you did send someone."

"I want to exclude that possibility."

"You say now that you definitely remember that you did not send anyone?"

"Of course, this is a very difficult matter. I have to think about this and it takes time to think it over, and I have thought about it, and I cannot remember any case. Therefore, nobody would have been sent."

"Well then, do you say definitely you did not send anyone to a concentration camp or recommend that anyone be sent to a concentration camp?"

"Well, I say I do not know of any case."

"Well, that means then you did not send anyone?"

"Yes."

"Why didn't you say that at the very beginning instead of putting us to all this trouble of questioning you to finally get that answer? Why did you first say you didn't remember?"

"I had no reason. I just wanted to be careful."

"Well, aren't you careful now?"

"Yes, I think I am."

"Well, tell us very definitely, did you or did you not, during the whole year that you were in charge of the state police, recommend that anyone be sent to a concentration camp?"

"As far as I know, no."

"Now, we are back to where we started from."

201

If Biberstein's answers professing a child's innocence to concentration camp commitments were incredulous, his replies to questions as to how he discharged his duties as a Gestapo chief were at least "wondrous strange." Having in mind the savage attitude of the Gestapo organization toward all those who dared to voice opposition to the Nazi regime, I asked Biberstein what he would do as a Gestapo chief if he learned that someone in his district had said he hoped Germany would lose the war because it was an unjust war anyway.

Essaying the voice of the most indulgent schoolma'am, he replied, "I would have asked the man to come to me and would have told him to hold onto his own views and keep them to himself and just would have warned him."

Giving the defendant the benefit of the doubt that there could be a moment that a Gestapo chief would forget his training, which taught him to crack the skull of anybody who said that Germany would not win the war, I now put a little stronger question. "You are on your way home one evening from the office and someone comes up to you and tells you that he overheard Hans Smith inveigh against the German Army, the German Government, Hitler and the whole National Socialist regime . . . What do you do?"

He replied, "Nobody would have done this, I don't think."

I said: "Well, let us suppose someone did. Peculiar things happen."

But even here, Biberstein would still be the indulgent schoolma'am. "I would have told him, 'Don't talk about it. Keep it to yourself, keep it quiet.'"

Since it was obvious now that Biberstein had determined to make himself the most indulgent, kind and sweet Gestapo chief that could ever be imagined, I increased the voltage of the provocative hypothesis. "Well let's go a little further. This man who stops you on your way home says, 'By the way, I just found out that there is a plot on here to kill Hitler. I heard the men talking about this; I know the house in which they gather; I saw some bombs being taken into the house and I want you to know about this, Herr Biberstein.' What would you do?"

Even this would not awaken the sleeping lion in Biberstein's breast. He replied, "I would have told him, 'Go to Official So and So and report it to him.'"

"And you would have done nothing?"

"Why, what could I have done? I didn't know what to do. I had no police directives."

I now summed up: "So your big job was to keep quiet, keep invisible, and avoid people telling you about plots against Hitler. That's the way you put in the whole year."

"Yes, about this plot against Hitler I don't quite understand. I said if anything like that came up I would have told this man who told me to report this to the police official. He would be interested in this."

"You would not be interested?"

"No, when I say, 'Go to him,' that is, then I had done everything that was necessary in my opinion because I can't arrest the people."

"And you would go home feeling fine and entirely content that you had done your duty to your Fuehrer?"

"Yes, the official would then deal with it. I wouldn't know what to do concerning police matters."

Although Biberstein was too considerate to send anyone to a concentration camp and of too forgiving a nature to arrest anyone who was plotting to kill Hitler, he somehow found no difficulty in adjusting his sensibilities to the point where he could witness two executions just for the experience of seeing people killed.

"You didn't know before you witnessed the execution

that you would have a feeling of revulsion against executions?

"Of course not, your Honor, for, before, I had never seen an execution."

"So you had to see an execution in order to know that it offended against your sentiments?"

"Yes, I had to see what kind of an effect this would have on me."

Biberstein not only witnessed these executions, but they were performed by his orders. He ordered many other executions. He said, however, that he never imposed the sentence of death without first being certain, by investigation or trial, that the victims were deserving of death.

For many hours on the witness stand he double-talked, evaded, denied and dissembled, his bustling brain ever seeking answers which would avoid incrimination and admission of guilt, but in a careless moment truth leaped the barrier of his conscious lips, and he openly confessed to murder.

Fifty persons were killed in the first execution he witnessed, fifteen in the second. I asked him whether he conducted investigations to determine the guilt or innocence of these sixty-five persons. He said that he did not see the files of these sixty-five cases, but he did know that he had given orders to his Kommando to investigate cases.

The interrogation continued. "You do not know of your own knowledge that these cases were investigated? These sixty-five deaths?"

"I did not see it."

"No. So, therefore, you permitted sixty-five people to go to their deaths without knowing yourself whether they were guilty or not?"

"I said that I only made spot checks."

This introduced something novel into the field of spot-checking. One may spot-check potatoes in a barrel to determine generally if they are fit for consumption, and a motion picture director could understandably spot-check every fifth "extra" to be certain that all the "extras" are wearing the proper costume for a certain scene. But to question or investigate only every fifth or sixth person in an assemblage of sixty-five to ascertain whether the entire sixty-five should be killed is a startling innovation in testing procedure. But as tragically inadequate as a spot check would be to save innocent persons from an unjust death, Biberstein did not accord these sixty-five fateful captives even that minimum of protection.

"Did you make any spot checks in these sixty-five?"

"Not among these sixty-five."

"Then we come back to the conclusion that you permitted sixty-five people to go to their death without even a spot check?"

"Without having made a spot check, yes."

Thus, Biberstein acknowledged in open court that he sent sixty-five persons to their death and watched them die with no evidence of guilt against them. The records, however, disclosed that he killed many more. Thousands of murders were on the soul of this man who, while admitting that his victims had souls, treated them as few human beings treat the most wretched beasts in the animal kingdom.

Since Biberstein had been a minister of the gospel, I asked him if he offered religious comfort to those he was about to kill. He replied that it would be "tasteless" to do so.

"Do you think it is bad taste at any time to talk about God?"

"No, your Honor."

"Well, now, here is a man who is going to be shot; he is going to be killed."

"Yes."

"He is going to pass out of existence. You are the pastor, or were a pastor. You are religiously trained. It didn't occur to you to say a comforting word to this individual who was starting on this long journey?"

"I had no opportunity to do this. If I describe this to you you may understand it, your Honor."

"Well, I am giving you a chance to describe it. You were the Kommando leader. Why didn't you have the opportunity to talk to these individuals and give them a word or two of comfort?"

"I could have got that opportunity any time, yes."

"Well, why didn't you do it?"

"Your Honor, if somebody had come to me I would not have rejected him, but to force myself on somebody, that is not my way."

"Well, would you be forcing yourself on an individual who is about to be executed, to tell him that he would soon be standing before his God, and to have strength in this final moment? Would it have been so difficult to do that?"

He explained that the prisoners were Bolshevists and "one should not throw pearls before swine."

"Did you think that because they were Bolshevists and had been fighting Germany that they did not have souls?"

"No."

"You did believe they had souls then, didn't you?"

"Of course."

"But because they were of the attitude which you have expressed, you did not think it was worth while to try to save these souls?"

206

"I had to assume that these were atheists. There are people who do not believe in God, who have turned away from God, and if I tell such a man a word of God, I run the danger that the person will become ironic."

"Well, suppose he did become ironic, that could not be any worse than the fact that he was going to be killed rather soon. Suppose he did become ironic, how did that harm anyone?"

"These things are too sacred to me that I would risk them in such situations."

He testified that he still had love for his fellow-man, and I asked him, "Do you think that you demonstrated that 'love of fellow-men' by letting these people go to their deaths without a word of comfort along religious lines, considering that you were a pastor? Did you demonstrate there a 'love of fellow-man?' "

And his unblushing answer was, "I didn't sin against the Commandments of Love."

A fairly good idea of Biberstein's concept of human love can be gained from his statement that as between inflicting death by firing squads and by means of the gas vans, he preferred using the latter because he found that the gas vans "were more pleasant for both parties."

It is astonishing how Biberstein and other defendants employed the name of the Deity in relating stories which could possibly hush in wonder the Ultimate Court when It considers the deeds of man on earth and the judgments to be pronounced. Ohlendorf, for instance, defined "freedom" as "the voluntary ties of the individual, the motives of his will and actions, the obvious will of God, in nature and history." The defendant Heinz Jost said, "The Jewish people have their right as a part of God's creation in exactly the way that the German people, too, have their right to live." The defendant Erwin Schulz said, "In my sacred duty to serve my Fatherland I never forgot my duty towards humanity." The defendant Adolf Ott was pleased to declare, "All my actions have been guided by reason and humane compassion." The defendant Walter Haensch declared, "Nobody can disturb the peace of my conscience."

I can still hear in my mind these voices and the voices of other defendants in Court uttering pious statements about God, conscience and humanity, as I recall the testimony with its narratives of events which extended deep into the realm of barbaric cruelty and unrestrained savagery.

CHAPTER FIFTEEN

IT IS TO BE DOUBTED THAT ONE COULD FIND AT A CASUAL table or in a corner of a public library as many educated people as were gathered in the defendants' dock of the Einsatzgruppen trial in Nuremberg. As chief of the stupendous "Jewish solution" program, Adolf Eichmann was satisfied to have the concentration camps with their extermination chambers run by rough characters like Rudolf Hoess who very rarely was seen in public. With the Einsatzguppen, however, things were different. The officers of this organization traveled continuously and should, therefore, carry the imprint of Nazi refinement into the various countries in which they appeared at the head of their action battalions.

Eichmann had gone far since the days in Linz when he lay in ambush with other lads and pounced on Jewish boys as they went by. His lifelong determination to bring disaster to all Jews was now operating on a grand scale of efficiency and culture. He therefore wanted at the head of the Einsatzgruppen not only men with a good academic education but men who had in some way or other made a mark in the higher intellectual and cultural life of the nation. We have seen that among his appointees captaining the various extermination units were lawyers, a university professor, an architect and an ex-minister. The list also included a graduate economist, a dental physician, a business man, a government clerk and an expert on art. The roll call was further embellished by the attention-arresting name of Heinz Hermann Schubert, who traced his ancestry back to kinship with the famous composer of the *Unfinished Symphony.*

In this interesting collection of human beings there was even a professional opera singer, SS-Major Waldemar Klingelhoefer, whose death-mask face could have allowed him to sing the part of Mephistopheles in *Faust* without make-up. The aria he sang in the Palace of Justice at Nuremberg, however, was hardly a melodious one. For two and a half years, Major Klingelhoefer had traveled martially with Einsatzgruppe B as this highly efficient slaying organization chanted its dirge of blood through Smolensk, Brest-Litowsk and other parts of western Russia. During this period the Gruppe killed tens of thousands of Jews, gypsies and "asocials."

Although Klingelhoefer did his part in upholding the vigor of the Fuehrer-Order under whose banner he marched and slew, he testified that he really felt an "inner reaction" against the order. What was the nature of this "inner reaction?" The episode of Tatarsk, a city one day's journey from Smolensk, answers the question. He testified that when he learned that thirty Jews had left the ghetto in Tatarsk and had returned to their homes without permission, he ordered them shot. The gasp of visitors in the courtroom at this impassive recital of killing people for going home seemed to stir Klingelhoefer into offering further explanation. He hastily added that before ordering the death of the thirty men he made an investigation and found that these men, through the intervention of three women, had given assistance to partisans. He was asked if he knew as a fact that the Jews had cooperated with the partisans. He replied that the men had had "mental contact" with partisans. I asked him if he meant by this that there had been no physical contact with the partisans.

He acknowledged that there had been no such contact. "Not physically but mentally, your Honor."

"Mentally, yes. And the only contact they had was through these three women?"

"Yes, through these three women."

"All right. So, therefore, the only evidence you had upon which to kill these thirty Jews was that they had mentally communicated with the partisans and they were in their homes mentally determined to resist you. That's the evidence you had, isn't it?"

That indeed was the evidence. And on this "evidence" he shot not only the thirty Jews but the three women as well. However, it must be said in his behalf that he did accord the women chivalrous courtesies. He said, "I gave the NCO the directive to separate these three women from the men to be shot, and to carry out the execution in an orderly manner. I asked the NCO to have them blindfolded, and that the women should be shot blindfolded."

He added a special concession. He had the women buried in a separate grave.

Of course, it is obvious that there was no justification whatsoever in law for this execution and that the victims were killed only because they were Jews. Under vigorous cross-examination by Chief Prosecutor Ferencz, Klingelhoefer finally conceded as much:

"Then whether he did or whether he did not violate

the directives he was killed. If he stayed in the Ghetto and if he left the Ghetto he was killed. If he contacted the partisans he was killed. If he did not contact the partisans he was killed. No matter what a Jew did he was killed, is that correct?"

"Yes."

Klingelhoefer was the man who led the expedition to obtain fur coats, an event already briefly mentioned. In describing this venture Klingelhoefer said that the Jews from whom he got the fur coats were arrested by order of Hauptsturmfuehrer Egon Noack, but that "the executions proper were carried out by Noack under my supervision." He said further that "it could be assumed that the Jews, owing to their good living conditions which they had in the USSR, possessed winter clothing; in fact, so much of it that a seizure for the purposes of the occupation forces would not matter to them very much."

In that statement he was undoubtedly correct because it could not matter "very much" to the Jews who were killed what was to later happen to their winter clothing.

Despite Klingelhoefer's alleged "inner reaction" against the Fuehrer-Order he served in the Einsatzgruppen for thirty months, making no effort to be relieved of his assignment.

"You never told Naumann that you wanted to get out of Einsatz Headquarters, did you?"

"No, because there would not have been much point in it. He would not have released me."

"How do you know he would not have released you?"

"I know that he would not release me. I knew that quite well because I was a special expert speaking Russian perfectly and knowing the conditions. Therefore he could not do without me."

An indication of Klingelhoefer's credibility can be

212

gathered from the following occurrence. Prior to the trial he had been interrogated by an Allied investigator, Mr. Wartenberg, and his replies had been reduced to writing. The transcript of that interrogation contained no reference to the three women he admitted at the trial he had killed. I inquired if Mr. Wartenberg hadn't asked him if he had killed women and children. He said that Mr. Wartenberg did ask him that question and that he told Wartenberg he did not kill women and children "on principle." He said he remembered this well because he had in his mind the "picture of the two hundred women and children" he had led back into the ghetto.

He spoke this with some bravado. I asked, "Did you remember the picture of the three women standing before these ten men out in the woods, ready to go to their Creator, with their graves dug close by? Did you remember that picture?"

He colored slightly and then, recovering self-assurance, explained that at the time of the interrogation he was excited. In addition, he said, he was depressed over the fact that Germany had lost the war. His testimony on this point is interesting:

"Would you have been very happy if the Reich had succeeded in its aims of the conquest of Europe?"

"Your Honor, I don't know whether the aims of the Reich were to make conquest of Europe. I don't know that. But of course, I would have been happy if Germany had won the war. That is quite natural."

"You would have been happy if Germany had won the war, even at the expense of its present condition—two million Germans killed, the nation in utter ruins, and all of Europe devastated. You would have been still happy if Germany had won the war?"

"Yes."

"Would you?"

"Yes, well, that is quite natural. That is a matter of course."

SS-First Lieutenant Heinz Hermann Schubert, who self-satisfiedly told us that he was a descendant of the illustrious composer Franz Schubert, wrote a tragic score for the *Marcia Funebre* played by Einsatzgruppe D in the Crimean Peninsula. He served as adjutant to Otto Ohlendorf from October, 1941, until July, 1942, and during that period lived the whole gamut of this organization's activities, since he handled its orders, assignments to executions, and reports to Berlin on the results attained.

Rather stalwart in appearance and wearing a military uniform adorned with a high velvet collar, he affected a startled attitude that he should be charged with anything at all suggestive of crime. His position in the Einsatzgruppe was only administrative, he said, and therefore no guilt could attach to him for what the organization did. But Schubert's guilt began when he voluntarily joined the lawless SD and SS which were committed to unrestrained felony, and his guilt intensified when he unprotestingly and willingly participated in the obviously criminal performances of Einsatzgruppe D.

While it cannot be legally questioned that the man in the robber gang who does the bookkeeping and enjoys the forbidden fruits of the gang's misdeeds is as guilty as those who hold up the banks, Schubert's lawyer argued that his client's case was different. He failed, however, to show how it was different. Schubert was not merely bookkeeper of an organization bent on violence and lawlessness without limit; he did not live in a paper world. He rode with the assassins in one of the biggest and strangest mass murders committed by Einsatzgruppe D —the massacre at Simferopol, which needs a description of its own.

One reads with uneasy spirit of the French Reign of Terror when the guillotine blade in the public square rose and fell like a village pump handle. One turns sadly the black pages of history recording the St. Bartholomew Massacre, the martyrdom of Christians in the Colisseum, and the Armenian Slaughter. To these melancholy classics of carnage must be added the Christmas of Simferopol, as described at the Einsatzgruppen trial in Nuremberg.

In the early part of December, 1941, the commander of the German Eleventh Army operating in the Crimea informed General Ohlendorf that it was his wish that the Jews and gypsies, of whom there were about ten thousand in Simferopol, be killed before Christmas. The order did not consternate Ohlendorf. On the mystic chords of memory no echo resounded in his ears of the Christmas carols he had heard in childhood, nor did he recall the message of Peace on Earth, Good Will toward Men. He transmitted the order to SS-Colonel Werner Braune, commanding Einsatzkommando 11B, who, also, saw nothing incongruous in the prospect of mingling blood with the evergreen of Christmas trees and the golden recollections of the yuletide. The only difficulty confronting Braune was that he lacked enough men and equipment for so accelerated an action. However, he would do his best. He called on the army commander and explained that he wished to abide by his wishes but that he needed some assistance. Could he have a few men, some extra rifles, and enough ammunition to finish off ten thousand people? The army commander saw nothing unreasonable in the request and gladly promised him enough personnel, trucks, rifles and cartridges to accomplish the job.

And it was done. By Christmas the Jews and gypsies, ten thousand of them, were lying in their graves.

In describing the operation, Colonel Braune almost cheerfully testified, "It took place under my responsibility. Once I was at the place of execution with Mr. Ohlendorf and there we convinced ourselves that the execution took place according to the directives laid down by Ohlendorf at the beginning of the assignment."

Prosecutor Walton wished to know why it was necessary that the slaughter be done before Christmas. Braune did not know exactly. "I wasn't able at the time to find out all the reasons. Maybe the reasons were strategic reasons; military reasons, which caused the Army to issue that order. Maybe they were territorial questions. Maybe they were questions of food."

It was enough for Braune that the men, women, and children should die. However, holding high the never-drooping standard of Einsatz gallantry, he saw to it that the killings were performed humanely, that is, humanely for the *executioners*. Lieutenant Schubert, who managed the gypsy sequence of the scenario, joined Braune in this splendid demonstration of humanitarianism.

He testified: "I know that it was of the greatest importance to Ohlendorf to have the persons who were to be shot killed in the most humane and military manner possible because otherwise—in other methods of killing—the moral strain (*seelische Belastung*) would have been too great for the execution squad."

He explained further: "I took care that the condemned persons were not beaten while the loading was going on." He also saw that the robbery of the victims would be accomplished without violence. Of course, he did not use the word "robbery." For him it was entirely legal. He phrased it in this manner: "I convinced myself that the

216

collection of money and valuables of people to be shot was not done by force, etc."

Schubert, also, did not know the reason for the Simferopol executions but he was satisfied that it was proper. "I did not know why the individuals were being executed. It is possible that there were persons among them who because of some special examination were being executed. As for me, in general, however, I was certain of one thing, that this was an execution based on the Fuehrer-Order."

At last the masterful job was done and Christmas was at hand, but the executioners were depressed, not because of the slaughter but because they now feared for their own lives. Braune testified that they apprehended the danger of falling into the hands of the Russians, now staging a counterattack. The grim death mask, behind which they had performed the gory deed with laboratory efficiency, now turned its ghastly features on them. Consternation reigned; the executioners' guns might be directed against the executioners. However, the danger passed, rubber knees straightened, and the relieved assassins gathered to jubilate on the most joyous day of Christendom. Since they were as defiant of God's commandments as they had been contemptuous of man's legal code, I wondered on what basis they celebrated the Natal Day of Christ. Braune said that over the food and drink Ohlendorf made a speech.

"And did he talk on religious matters?"

"I cannot give any details of the words any more. I don't know whether he mentioned Christ, but I know Herr Ohlendorf's attitude on all this."

"What was his attitude as he delivered his speech? What did he say that was of religious significance?"

"Your Honor, I really cannot give any details any more."

217

"Did anybody offer any prayers on Christmas Day of 1941?"

"Your Honor, I do not know. . . ."

"Were any prayers offered for the thousands of Jews that you had just killed. . . . ?"

"Your Honor, I don't know whether anyone prayed for these thousands of Jews."

Schubert also did not know whether anyone had prayed for the Jews and the gypsies who were slain. He did remember specifically, however, just how the killing was done. He testified with a stoicism which harmonized with his awesome uniform, but which clashed with the tender sentiment his illustrious name inevitably evoked. He told how the executioners fired their rifles and machine pistols at the heads of the doomed who, receiving the shots, toppled into the ditches by which they stood.

No matter how often these terrible scenes were described I always ached inwardly at the horror of them, but what perennially froze my blood was the realization of the possibility that some victims did not die at once but fell into the ditches alive, and then only slowly expired in agony, pain, terror, loneliness and despair covered with dirt, water and other bodies, blinded by pain, tormented by desolation, and tortured by the realization of what man can do to man.

I asked Schubert, "Do you exclude the possibility that a rifleman might have aimed badly and as a result the victim would receive only a shock; he could have been knocked unconscious by the bullet but not actually be dead so that to the casual observer he would seem to be dead although in fact his heart was still beating?"

"Your Honor, I cannot exclude such a possibility."

Schubert knew that the killings were based on the Fuehrer-Order and he knew that the Fuehrer-Order di-

218

rected a gargantuan crime. He was part of that crime, but his attorney, Dr. Koessel, in presenting Schubert's case to the Tribunal, argued there was nothing criminal about his action. "What did Schubert actually do which was criminal?" the attorney asked. And then he answered his own question: "Schubert first goes to the gypsy quarter of Simferopol and sees them being loaded aboard and shipped off. Then he drives to the place of execution, sees the rerouting of traffic, the roads blocked off, persons being unloaded, valuables handed over, and the shooting. Finally he drives back once more along the way to the gypsy quarter and there again sees them being loaded aboard and carried off, and then returns to his office. That is what he did."

Dr. Koessel's argument brought to mind Pope's quatrain

> Vice is a monster of so frightful a mien,
> As to be hated needs but to be seen;
> Yet seen too oft, familiar with her face,
> We first endure, then pity, then embrace.

In preparing Schubert's defense, Dr. Koessel apparently came so close to the Einsatzgruppen and became so familiar with its face that he failed to see the malignity in its every action. What had Schubert done that was wrong? He had directed an execution of human beings who happened to be gypsies; there was no assertion anywhere that these gypsies were guilty of anything but being gypsies. He had made every effort to have the massacre conducted clandestinely; he had controlled the shuttling of twenty-five trucks which loaded the gypsies at the assembly site, transported them to the field of death, and returned for fresh loads. He had directed the despoliation of their private property and then had "supervised the actual shooting." He also admitted that he would have intervened if things were not going "well."

And yet Koessel asked, What is wrong about that? Koessel failed to realize that Schubert was taking an active part in mass murder—a mass murder in which he not only helped with the planning but took an active part in its sanguinary fulfillment.

CHAPTER SIXTEEN

SS-MAJOR WALDEMAR VON RADETZKY WAS ANOTHER DE-
fendant who not only denied having killed Jews but insisted he did not even know that Jews were being killed.
Von Radetzky served for fifteen months with Sonderkommando 4A, the unit headed by Paul Blobel, who made
of it during his incumbency one of the goriest in the
history of the Einsatzgruppen. Von Radetzky's explanation for his ignorance of all this bloodletting was that
he devoted his entire time to writing reports. Of course,
reports were indeed prepared. In fact, the prosecution's
case was mostly based on reports made by Einsatz leaders. But Von Radetzky said his reports had nothing to do
with executions since he was interested only in the scenic,
cultural, and economic aspects of the country in which
his organization operated. One might assume, if Von
Radetzky were to be believed, that his Kommando was
engaged in a scientific expedition studying the flora and
fauna of the land, gathering data on agriculture and
economy, and somehow forgetting the homicidal under-
taking to which it was committed under the Fuehrer-
Order.

Since Radetzky was the next highest ranking officer to Blobel in Sonderkommando 4A, did it not occur to him to ask why blood was seeping in under his tent or why so much of it besmeared the landscape which he studied for his reports on vegetation?

In an effort to minimize his importance in this mass-killing business, Radetzky testified that he was brought into Einsatzgruppe C as an interpreter because he was born in Moscow and therefore knew the Russian language. Later, however, he said that since his Kommando operated in the Ukraine he was of no use as an interpreter. He testified that he reported on agriculture, industry, trade and "cultural questions." "My main attention went to questions of economy because that was something I knew something about."

I asked him if, in reporting on economy, he would have to know about the Jews. He replied that he did know about them.

"And when you reported on economy you had to report on the Jews who were being executed, didn't you?"

"No, your Honor."

"If the Jews in any given territory were executed, it would seriously affect the economy of that territory, wouldn't it?"

"Your Honor, the whole economy of the Ukraine was in a very bad state, at that time."

"Please answer the question. If the Jews were executed in any given territory, that mere fact would have a very grave effect on the economy, wouldn't it?"

"Certainly, your Honor."

"Then in making a report on the economy you would have to say: 'Because of the depletion of the labor supply due to the execution of Jews, a certain situation has resulted.' You would have to say that, wouldn't you?"

"Your Honor, all these questions concerning Jews were merely the sphere of activities of Departments 3 and 4, and I did not report about these activities."

"You did not answer my question. Making a report on the economy you would naturally have to talk about labor, and if a great number of those constituting the labor element were executed, that would affect seriously the economy of the country on which you were reporting, and you would need to include that in your reports, would you not?"

"The situation which we found, your Honor, was that the entire economy had been ruined and had to be built up. There was no shop in which you could buy anything."

"The economy wasn't helped by shooting off further labor supply, was it?"

"No."

"Did you make this statement in your reports, that because Jews were being killed—and the labor market was thereby being affected adversely—that the economy was made worse? Did you report that?"

"As far as I remember I reported about the fact that the Jews in the Ukraine constituted an essential part of trade."

"And did you report that Jews were being decimated?"

"No, your Honor."

"You didn't put in any report that Jews were being decimated?"

"No, your Honor."

"You didn't put in any report that Jews were being killed and this affected the economy of the Ukraine?"

"No, in this shape I did not report about it. I only reported about the fact that the Jews were an important economic potential, but I did not report to the effect as you mention it."

"You say that you reported that the Jews were an important economic potential and you say that you did include in your report the statement that the Jews constituted an important economic potential. Did you then add that this important economic potential was rapidly disappearing because of the executions?"

"No, your Honor, I did not report that."

"And yet you want to tell the Tribunal seriously that you made a report on the economy of the Ukraine?"

Without the slightest abashment and without any attempt at a long explanation he affirmed with a single, categorical "Yes."

Although he had begun his testimony with the statement that he was brought into the Einsatzgruppen because of his knowledge of languages, he now saw from documents which had been introduced in evidence that the interpreter's role would not necessarily isolate him from knowledge of executions, because executions very frequently followed investigations in which interpreters were used. Thus, although he finally admitted that he spoke and understood the Ukrainian language, he said that he was not called upon to translate during examinations because his work day was filled up with the job of being an expert in the SD, which was department III.

"Well, how did you become an expert in the department III? You had not had SD training."

"No, I did not have that, your Honor. I said——"

"Well then, how did you become an expert so quickly?"

"I was appointed for this because of my training in economics and my knowledge of languages."

"Well now, we come back to languages again. If you were appointed because of your linguistic accomplishments and your commanding officer needed an interpreter, why wouldn't he naturally turn to you who were already known to be a good translator and interpreter?"

224

"Your Honor, there were other interpreters in the Kommando, and the Commander used these interpreters."

"Then you were not used as an interpreter?"

"I was never used as interpreter by the Commander. I was never used in interrogations as interpreter either."

Since Radetzky was an interpreter who did not interpret and a report writer who made no report on executions (the principal activity of his organization), he perhaps felt obliged to explain how he put in his time. He offered to fill in the hiatus by stating that he was supply officer, obtaining food and fuel for the Sonderkommando. I asked him if he also ordered the ammunition used by his unit. He replied, "I don't remember."

"If you remember food and fuel, you can remember whether you ordered ammunition or not. Did you order ammunition?"

"No, your Honor."

He saw, of course, that an admission on ammunition would be an admission of knowledge about executions.

"Do you remember now very definitely that you did not order ammunition?"

"Yes."

"Why did you say just a minute ago that you did not remember?"

"Your Honor, perhaps my expression was misused or came through the wrong way. I said I did not remember ever having requested ammunition."

"Well, that is the way it came through. Now, do you or do you not remember having ordered ammunition for your kommando?"

"No."

. . . "Do you say now definitely that you did not order ammunition?"

"Your Honor, I am certain that I would remember if ever I had obtained ammunition for the kommando."

225

"And you say you did not order ammunition?"

And now, apparently in order to play it completely safe, he answered both ways: "No—yes."

One of the reports (not Radetzky's) described a conference held between officers of Sonderkommando 4A and those of rear military headquarters on September 10, 1941, where a decision was reached to "liquidate the Jews of Zhitomir radically." As a result of this conference 3154 Jews were executed. Radetzky denied having attended the conference but admitted that he supplied trucks for the action which he said he thought was for "resettlement" of the Jews in Rowno. It did not require a doctor of philosophy of Professor Six's education to know that when the word "resettlement" was mentioned in connection with Jews, it meant liquidation. Prosecutor Horlik-Hochwald questioned Radetzky.

"What happened to these Jews in Rowno?"

"According to the order which I received at the time it said that they would be resettled there."

"Were they to be killed there, Mr. Radetzky?"

"Nothing was said about this."

"Is it not a little illogical? We have just discussed a document a few minutes ago which shows that the Jews in Rowno were killed and now you tell the Tribunal that in order to get new Jews in Rowno they were to be sent from Zhitomir and don't you think that this is a little bit illogical?"

"Mr. Prosecutor, I on my part always hoped that this problem would be regulated differently than it was regulated in other cases."

Radetzky's mental acrobatics on the witness stand were phenomenal to behold. In meeting his insistence that he never commanded an execution unit, the prosecution introduced an official document taken from Einsatzgruppen personnel files which spoke of Radetzky's promotion. It also carried the statement, "During the advance, in the summer of 1942, SS-Hauptfuehrer von Radetzky was put in command of a 'Teilkommando.'" Radetzky said that the document correctly reported his promotion but incorrectly reported his commanding a Teilkommando.

"How can you explain that it could be so accurate and so prophetic as to bring about your promotion as of the ninth of September. . . . and yet it be incorrect insofar as the statement about your commanding a Teilkommando?"

"Your Honor, I do not say that it is a mistake; I say it is an error, and I must try to clarify this error."

". . . The hairbreadth distinction between a mistake and an error is one which requires stronger glasses than I use. Now, tell me, what is the difference between a mistake and an error?"

"A mistake is an absolute incorrectness and an error is, in my opinion, an involuntary incorrectness, that is, a mistaken representation."

Radetzky was clever enough to realize that his shifting answers, evasive responses, and purposeful distortions of intent, when persisted in at length, could not increase his credibility. Perhaps, then, in an effort to add measure to his dwarfing figure of believability, he said that it was impossible that he could have participated in a program of racial extermination since he was a humane person. To prove this postulate he said that when his Kommando was stationed at Charkov in the Ukraine he had brought in three hundred tons of food to save the starving population in that city. I asked him, "Did any of this food go to any Jewish family?"

"Yes, certainly."

"Did you see it being served to any Jewish family?"

"I did not see a family at all who received such supplies."

"Well, how do you know that any Jews received this supply?"

"Because I know that the entire population received food."

"Well, you know also that Jews were being killed, don't you? You know that, don't you?"

"No, I did not know that."

"You do not know that Jews were being killed?"

"I know that Jews were killed, but . . ."

"All right, do you want to tell us that first you would feed them and then shoot them?"

"I don't know anything about it, your Honor; therefore, I can't say anything about it."

Taking up his claim that he was a person of humane impulses I asked him if he did not know that Jews were being persecuted in his area. He said he did know this but when I asked him, "You knew that they were having a harder time to live than anybody else?" he hedged. "Whether conditions were more severe than conditions for others, I do not know. I would doubt that, because the town was near to starvation."

However, when I followed with "Well, you knew that they were being killed. That is about as much as you can do to a person, isn't it?" he replied, "Yes."

Although he had insisted that his job was to report to Berlin on all conditions he found in the area traversed by his Kommando, he did not include the feeding item in his report.

"When you made your report to Berlin, did you say that you helped to feed Jews in Charkov?"

"No, your Honor."

"Did you say that Jews were being fed in Charkov?"

"No, your Honor."

"Can you honestly say today that you know of your

own personal knowledge that one Jew received any of this food that you spoke about in Charkov—from your own personal knowledge?"

"According to my own personal knowledge and experience, I cannot say that. I can only say that I urged the administrative bodies that the whole population should receive this food."

However, despite all his equivocations, inventions, and circumlocutions, Radetzky finally had to admit, under the persevering cross-examination of Prosecutor Horlik-Hochwald, that he was thoroughly familiar with the Fuehrer-Order and that he was an active participant in its ruthless program.

The parents of Lothar Fendler fondly hoped that he would devote his life to preserving the teeth of his fellow-Germans through the practice of dentistry and sent him to school with that objective in mind. However, at twenty-one years of age, Lothar, having grown quite tall, decided that he would look better in an officer's uniform than a dentist's smock, and accordingly joined the army. In May, 1941, he became an SS major and the second highest ranking officer in Sonderkommando 4A of Einsatzgruppe C which carried the force and the glory of the Fuehrer-Order into Lemberg, Tarnopol, Winnitza, Uman, Kirowograd, Krementschuk and Poltawa, in most of which places executions occurred. Like von Radetzsky, Fendler testified he knew nothing of these killings since he was writing reports on the morale of the people in the territory through which his unit passed.

He also said that he only learned of executions by accident and knew nothing of the Fuehrer-Order until he had left the Kommando and was on his way home.

"So that you had to travel five hundred kilometers and

two days' distance from the very heart of this execution district before you learned that executions were being performed upon Jews because they were Jews, is that right?"

Without batting an eyelash, he replied, "Yes."

It is simply not to be believed that Fendler could not be aware of the blood in the fields through which he tramped and in the streets over which his vehicle moved. An Einsatz action report dated July 11, 1941, stated that "Einsatzkommando 4B has finished its activity in Tarnopol. 127 executions. Parallel to that, liquidation of 600 Jews in the course of the persecutions of Jews is induced by the Einsatzkommando." It was impossible for Fendler to have been insulated from knowledge of what occurred in the very city in which he was stationed. And only blindness, combined with deafness and paralysis, could have hidden from him knowledge of the pogrom which was instigated by the Kommando in which he ranked second from the top command. Moreover, even at his own word about writing reports on morale, he could not help but know that the social atmosphere of Tarnopol had been violently rent by the explosion of a pogrom. Nevertheless, he said that he made no mention in his report of this butchering in the streets familiar to his eye. "Why didn't you make a report on these excesses which you learned about?"

"Because I personally did not get a chance."

"Why didn't you get a chance to make a report?"

"Because I was busy with another task, namely to evaluate the documents which had been captured."

"And you didn't consider the matter of a mass murder of six hundred people of sufficient importance to write a report on; is that what you are telling the Tribunal?"

"Your Honor, if I get the order from the Kommando

leader to evaluate the material which is available there, then I have to do so."

"Well, how much time would it take, in an SD report, which you were compelled to make, and which it was your job to make, to say that there were excesses in Tarnopol to the extent that six hundred Jews were murdered, or if you didn't want to say murdered, were killed by the population. How much time would it take to include that, with your fingers on the typewriter, into a report? How much time would it take to say that?"

"Two seconds."

"Well then, why didn't you have the two seconds to write that?"

"Because I made no report."

SS-Captain Felix Ruehl, perhaps the tallest of the defendants, was still one more Einsatz officer who bent low and kept his nose buried in papers, ledgers, and statistics amidst the clamor and clatter of rifle volleys, the smell of gunpowder, and the screams of people being shot in the towns on whose morale, industry and culture he was reporting to Berlin. But Sonderkommando 10B, Einsatzgruppe D, of which Ruehl sought (at the trial) to be recorded only as a literary member, was not an organization bent on cultural objectives. Document No. 4135 related that Sonderkommando 10B "finished its tasks at Chotin. Intellectually leading persons from the Soviet Party and public life, Jewish agitators, teachers, lawyers and rabbis were apprehended with the help of Ukrainian confidential agents in the course of several raids and treated accordingly." Of course "treated accordingly" was merely a sarcastic synonym for "shot to death."

Ruehl, who was administrative officer of his unit, testified that his duties consisted of office administration, billeting, food supply, personnel and motor vehicles. Therefore, he said, executions were entirely foreign to him. He admitted that he had been with his unit in the city of Chernowitz for a whole month. Prosecutor Walton asked him how the Kommando had put in its time there. He replied that "this stay was used mainly for taking up contact with the Russian and the Ukrainian Army and to become acquainted with conditions."

Was this statement credible? Would a Sonderkommando under the command of the inexorable, restless killer Ohlendorf remain in a large city of from three hundred thousand to four hundred thousand inhabitants only to become acquainted with conditions? Well, Ruehl did do something else. He helped to repair hotels! ". . . In addition, and this was the case especially in Chernowitz, there were the repairs of the hotels which had been assigned to us by the Romanian army, which the Russians had left in a very poor condition, as well as caring for Romanian, Hungarian and German guests."

After an extensive cross-examination by Prosecutor Walton, the defendant did admit that he learned of one execution: "Soon after my arrival in Chernowitz I learned by casual remarks by comrades that Romanian units, as well as members of our Kommando, when they moved into the city after the city had been taken, had been shot at by civilians. The Romanians had arrested a number of suspects and the Kommando had received the order to execute these people because of this incident."

Ruehl's armor-plated inperviousness to illegality was made manifest by his casual remark that "suspects" had been arrested and his Kommando had killed them.

That Ruehl, who was only fourth ranking officer in the Kommando, could not have done anything to prevent the recorded executions, is believable, but his assertion that as a member of a unit made up of only seven officers and eighty-five men he could not know that killings were taking place was even more fantastic than the demon's land in which his organization had been actually operating.

While the reports and the testimony at the trial decisively refuted Ruehl's assertions of ignorance of executions, they still did not rise to that degree of proof which Anglo-American procedure requires in order to support a verdict of guilty. We declared at the outset and adhered to the principle throughout the trial that every defendant would be presumed innocent until proved guilty and that no defendant would be convicted unless the evidence established his guilt beyond a reasonable doubt. We were not satisfied from the evidence in Ruehl's case that he was guilty of participation in executions beyond a reasonable doubt, or that he exercised sufficient authority to prevent them. We thus found him not guilty of war crimes and crimes against humanity, as outlined in the indictment, but guilty of membership in the criminal organizations SS and Gestapo under the conditions defined by the Judgment of the International Military Tribunal.

CHAPTER SEVENTEEN

DURING THE CROSS-EXAMINATION OF FELIX RUEHL, PROSE-
cutor Walton asked him if his commanding officer, Alois
Pesterer, was not addicted to alcoholic beverages. Thinking that the prosecution was attempting to equate criminality with intoxication, I ruled that I would not permit
that type of questioning. However, it developed that Mr.
Walton had another purpose in mind, namely, to prove
that Pesterer was at times so drunk that the control of
the Kommando had to be taken over by the defendant
Ruehl. Ruehl indignantly denied the suggestion that his
commander (now dead) had ever been drunk and then
undoubtedly, without realizing its tremendous significance in the case, said, "I strongly object to that in the
interest of the deceased. And I can assure you that if such
a thing had occurred even once, Herr Ohlendorf wouldn't
have stood for this. That would have been the end of
his career as a Kommando leader, insofar as I got to
know Herr Ohlendorf."

In Ruehl's answer can be found another answer to
critics who have insisted that at Nuremberg military men
were punished simply for obeying superior orders. According to Captain Ruehl, any Einsatz officer opposed to

slaughtering helpless innocent populations and seeking a way out of his dilemma could find that hoped-for way, if no more reasonable and courageous avenue was open to him, through the throat of a bottle of schnaps.

But one did not need to be branded a drunken sot, even temporarily, in order to refuse the role of murderer. A frank statement of incapacity to play the part of a hangman would have effected a release from the assignment. The Nazi hierarchy was cruel and even sadistic, but it could never have been charged with inefficiency in the execution of its inhuman deeds. Kommando leaders who demonstrated themselves incapable of performing cold-blooded slaughter were assigned to other duties, not out of sympathy or for humanitarian reasons, but for efficiency's sake alone. Ohlendorf had declared, as already stated, that he forbade the participation in executions of men who did not "agree to the Fuehrer-Order," and sent them back to Germany. In fact, Ohlendorf, as we saw earlier, could himself have shaken off the potential bloody knapsack of ninety thousand murders by simply disagreeing with the army commander dominating his field of operation.

In this respect, it is interesting to note the testimony of the witness Albert Hartel, who served with the German Security Police in Kiev. He testified that SS-General Thomas, commanding Einsatzgruppe C at the time, "passed on an order that all those people who could not reconcile with their conscience to carry out such orders, that is, people who were too soft, as he said, to carry out these orders, should be sent back to Germany or should be assigned to other tasks. Thus at the time a number of people, also commanders, were sent back by Thomas to the Reich just because they were too soft to carry out orders."

Prosecutor Walton questioned Hartel: "If Thomas

235

would have known, he would have sent a commander home, is that correct?"

"He would have sent him home saying that he was too soft. In a number of cases this happened, that Thomas actually sent these people back to Germany."

Thus, it certainly was not enough for a defendant to say, as did Braune and Klingelhoefer, that it was pointless to ask to be released and that therefore they did not even try. Exculpation is not so easy as that. The failure to attempt disengagement from an obviously criminal task can only prompt the conclusion that the person involved has no deep-seated desire to be released. He may think the work unpleasant but he nevertheless has a personal reason for performing it. Even a professional murderer may not relish killing his victim but he accomplishes the job in an efficient and workmanlike manner because of the reward which awaits him.

In fulfilling Hitler's program every Nazi official saw for himself a higher rank, a gaudier uniform, an easier and more lucrative post, a bigger and shinier car, an increased authority, a longer strut, and a more numerous group of underlings to tremble before his greatness. Vanity, arrogance, and greed were the vehicles in which the Nazi leaders traveled the highway of criminality and inhumanity. Equipped with the goggles of glory and gore, they saw nothing wrong in mass murder, pillage, thievery, kidnapping, torture, and diabolical destruction.

The Einsatzgruppen officers had an additional reason for preferring their assignments: it saved them from hazardous combat service. In the front lines one faced an armed and aggressive opponent; in a foxhole one could expect any moment a fragmentizing artillery shell. But on the Einsatzgruppen field there were no foxholes. There were only long ditches in front of which one's adversaries helplessly stood to await the fire which they could not return.

It can be assumed without forced reasoning that if, in the entire Einsatzgruppen history, any officer or soldier had been drastically punished because of refusal to obey the Fuehrer-Order, the defendants, who, in their collective experience, covered every Einsatz phase, would certainly have known about it. Yet throughout the seven months' trial there was no evidence that a failure to obey the Fuehrer-Order precipitated any major penalty. On the contrary, several instances came to light showing that disobedience or evasion of the Fuehrer-Order invoked no grievous punishment.

It will be recalled that Nosske said that if he had been ordered to shoot five hundred innocent Jews he would have had to do it. He later testified to the following episode. Upon returning to Germany after his Einsatz service in the East, he was assigned to duty in Düsseldorf where his higher SS and Police Leader ordered him to round up all Jews and *half-Jews* in that area for executions. Nosske said that he protested the order and that, finally, it was revoked, or at any rate not enforced. Nosske's protest was probably due mostly to the fact that many of the intended victims had one German parent. Nonetheless, his categorical refusal to obey the order demonstrated (contrary to the defense advanced throughout the trial) that a member of the German Armed Forces could protest a superior order and not be shot in consequence. Though it is true the defendant suffered some inconveniences because of his unwillingness to shoot the half-Jews of Düsseldorf, he was not shot or even degraded.

One who is ordered to commit a patently barbarous deed and refuses to do so may undergo some inconvenience because of that refusal, but he still has the duty to suffer that inconvenience rather than inflict an irreparable injustice upon one utterly innocent of wrongdoing. And then, aside from the moral issue involved, the person who submits himself to a slight or even great inconvenience, or even some temporary harm, will in the end fare better than the one who commits the barbarity, if they are later both called upon to answer for what they have done.

And thus, we come to a discussion of Mathias Graf, who served in Einsatzkommando 6, of Einsatzgruppe C, for thirteen months. His rank was that of Oberscharfuehrer (master sergeant). In September, 1942, he was assigned to the command of a sub-Kommando but he refused to accept the post. Because of this refusal he was arrested and placed in custody for disciplinary action. Eventually the disciplinary proceedings were dropped and he was sent back to Germany.

This defendant, who apparently was not a fanatical adherent of National Socialism, joined the SS in 1933, but in 1936 he was expelled because of lack of attendance and general indifference. In January, 1940, he was drafted under the Emergency Service Regulations for service with the Landrat and he then entered the SD on a war supplementary basis. We found him not guilty of war crimes and crimes against humanity and although he had served in the SD, we held that he had more than expiated this offense by his period of imprisonment prior to trial. Accordingly he was discharged on the day of our decision.

Every one of the defendants would have been entitled to an acquittal or at least to a considerable mitigation of penalty if he had responded to the Fuehrer-Order as Mathias Graf did. But the records, the testimony and the incontrovertible evidence at the trial all proved, on

238

the contrary, that the other defendants (minus Ruehl) eagerly accepted the Fuehrer-Order and avidly reflected the Fuehrer's hatred for Jewry. It is true that many of the defendants, at the trial, denied harboring racial prejudices. In fact, some of them stated that in Germany they often befriended the persecuted Jew. Under the liberal rules of procedure which we instituted, these defendants submitted affidavits from others demonstrating their generous conduct towards individual Jews in the fatherland.

But if it were true that the defendants regarded the Jews as equals in Germany, why did they consider them subhuman outside of Germany? If they did not recognize them as a mortal danger to Hitler in Germany, why should they regard them as such a threat in the Crimea? It is not too much to say that most of the Jews in Crimea and the other far reaches of the East did not know of Hitler and his doctrines until the Einsatzgruppen arrived to kill them.

It was argued in behalf of the defendants that even if they had refused to obey the Fuehrer-Order, or, in some manner, had avoided it, no substantial benefits would have accrued to the Jews, because the successors of the defecting Einsatz leaders would have conducted executions. But no defendant could predict what the next Kommando leader would have done. The successor could also have manifested his reluctance and thus, with continuing refusals, the Fuehrer-Order might well have lost its efficacy. But in any event there would have been no executions on the day of the refusal.

Repeatedly the German defense lawyers quoted the maxim *Nulla poena sine lege*, but the German law itself authorizes criminal responsibility for executing illegal

239

orders. Article 47 of the German Military Penal Code provides that

> If through the execution of an order pertaining to the service, a penal law is violated, then the superior giving the order is alone responsible. However, the obeying subordinate shall be punished as accomplice:
> (1) if he went beyond the order given to him, or
> (2) if he knew that the order of the superior concerned an act which aimed at a civil or military crime or offense.

CHAPTER EIGHTEEN

WHEN, IN HIS OPENING STATEMENT TO THE TRIBUNAL, CHIEF Prosecutor Ferencz spoke of the killing of thirty-three thousand Jews in Kiev in two days, he said that this feat stood out "even among the ghastly records of the Einsatzgruppen." Sonderkommano 4A, which, under the direction of Blobel, was responsible for most of these killings, formed part of Einsatzgruppe C, headed by SS-Brigadier General Otto Rasch, recognized wherever he appeared as one of the most brutal executants of Hitler's extermination program, often appearing personally on the field of execution to supervise the slaughter. Under Rasch's leadership Einsatzgruppe C acquired such a reputation for bloodthirstiness that, as Mr. Ferencz phrased it, "it shamed some of the German witnesses and the Einsatzgruppe had to report that 'Unfortunately it often occurred that the Einsatzkommandos had to suffer more or less hidden reproaches for their consequent stand on the Jewish problem.' "

Following the war, General Otto Rasch became crippled with Parkinson's Disease. He was well enough to attend the first sessions of the trial but when it was his turn to testify he was incapable of locomotion. However,

241

through his attorney, he expressed a desire to appear in court to defend himself, even though he had to be carried into the courtroom on a stretcher. Then, after he had been helped into the witness box, an army doctor stood by to keep the Tribunal informed on his condition so that we could recess court at any moment the doctor advised the defendant should not continue.

Raising his hand, which quivered in a slight arc, Rasch spoke the oath in a firm voice: "I swear by God, the Almighty and Omniscient, that I will speak the pure truth and will withhold and add nothing." Then, assuming a somewhat reclining position, he responded to the questions put by his attorney, Dr. Surholt. After informing the Court that he was born in East Prussia on December 7, 1891, and that his father was a farmer who later became a brick manufacturer he said, "My father was well to do. Seen from a sociological standpoint, he belonged to the patriarchal order . . . My father considered it his uppermost duty to take care of every one of his people. This social duty came from the deeper moral awareness from religion." He stopped, exhibiting fatigue. The doctor examined him and let him rest lying down.

Then, once more in the witness box, Rasch began to speak to the Court with the apparent comfort and contentment of one who, at his own fireside, is surrounded by grandchildren and their young friends who are listening absorbedly to the life story of an old and revered man. He related, with some emphasis, as if this was to be the motif of his paternal lecture, "At home I was educated very devoutly. That was in accord with the almost pious devoutness of my parents." Then, lifting his eyes in obviously fond reminiscence, he proudly recalled, "My father taught me the love of my country, love of nature, and how to hunt."

Who, good or bad, does not savor the delights which memory offers in recalling the days of carefree childhood? Rasch paused again. With one shaking hand he tried to still the shaking of the other, and again resumed, his face illumined by the picture his words were evidently evoking. "Very early in my life he took me along on his trips and above all he taught me the moral principles of hunting. He taught me that hunting was not just shooting and killing of game but it was also the care of and respect for the Creator and His creatures."

I asked him what he meant by the "moral principles of hunting" and he explained: "Hunting in the German sense demanded that the individual, even if he is completely unobserved in his area, realizes his obligations toward the creatures, and that he is to refrain from everything which violates these, for example shooting during the time it is prohibited—that is, during the time the animals are protected—shooting of the mother as long as her young ones need her, and only shooting on careful deliberation—not to satisfy one's passion for it."

Those in the courtroom who had heard the presentation of the reports, which told of the seventy-five thousand killings Rasch had ordered and of the misery he had inflicted on mankind, would have wanted him to explain why—after learning not to shoot animals beyond the hunting season, and particularly not to shoot the mothers of young animals—why it was that he grew up to enjoy shooting mothers of human children and the children themselves. Still, everyone must have felt sorry for this wreck of a man whose hands were now fluttering like aspen leaves. The listeners looked on him with pity and commiseration but still hoped that he might explain how it was that after being taught how to show "respect for the Creator and His creatures," he could manifest such violent disrespect for the fellow-creatures of his own human race.

But Dr. Surholt left this subject and asked the defendant about his education. "Do you have any special memories from this time which are important in your life?"

"I was a good student and I was on friendly terms with most of my teachers. I enjoyed a relationship of confidence with them. This lasted during my entire life."

He continued the story of his life until he got to telling about being private secretary to a Count zu Dona who would take him on many trips, including one to Paris, but fatigue now set in once more and we recessed Court to allow him to recuperate his strength. After several hours' rest and examination by a couple of doctors he came back into Court.

We said to him, "According to Anglo-American procedure, every defendant is presumed innocent until proved guilty beyond a reasonable doubt. You therefore stand before the court as an innocent man. You have been charged with crime, very serious crime, and the Tribunal is required to give you every opportunity to answer these charges. Thus, you are brought into court, not with the thought of subjecting you to an unpleasant and uncomfortable experience, but rather to a pleasant and comforting one in that at last you will have the opportunity to speak to the world."

Dr. Surholt acknowledged that his client was before the Court voluntarily but expressed doubt he could adequately meet the situation. I picked up the indictment. "Dr. Surholt, you will admit that any person charged with seventy-five thousand murders should be given every opportunity to exculpate himself even at the expense of physical discomfort . . . We want to make this very clear so that no one may get the impression that the defendant is being treated with but little compassion. There is the greatest of sympathy for his physical condition . . ." but, we went on to explain that with the grave charges enumerated in the indictment, the defendant unquestionably wanted to be heard, and it was his inherent right to be heard. Dr. Surholt agreed with this view, but it soon became apparent that his client simply was unable to muster sufficient strength to testify further. I suspended proceedings and ordered him removed to the hospital.

As an army sergeant and soldier took hold of the stretcher on which he was laid and a doctor walked by his side as they left the courtroom, I felt the need to cough. Something seemed to have lodged in my throat. Possibly it was the sheer melancholy of contemplating the picture of this ruin of a human being who could speak with the compassion of a St. Francis in behalf of the animals of the forest, but who could outdo the most ferocious beast of the jungle in massacring his fellow man.

Eventually we ordered his case severed from the present trial with the proviso that he was to be retried in the event he recovered. However, before he could give an accounting in Nuremberg or elsewhere for what he had done as an Einsatz general, he was summoned to the High Court for judgment on his whole life. He died November 1, 1948.

I do not doubt that Rasch told the truth about his early training. His father had indeed provided him with an excellent education. After attaining the degrees of Doctor of Jurisprudence and Doctor of Law and Economics he went on to practice law and then became mayor of Wittenberg. Certainly it cannot be said that it was lack of education which blinded Rasch to the evils and malevolence of the Nazi Party which he joined at the mature age of forty. So fortified was Rasch with degrees and academic accomplishments that sometimes he was addressed as "Dr. Dr." Nor can it be said of the other defendants that they were not intellectually equipped to decide for themselves what constituted decency and what spelled out infamy. So far as criminal conduct is concerned, it probably can be said (with deep regret) that the defendants' extensive education made them all the more capable and efficient in the discharge of their diabolical enterprises.

The great problem which I personally faced in the Einsatzgruppen trial was not in reaching a decision on the guilt or innocence of the defendants. That question began to resolve itself as the trial neared its end. What troubled me as a human being was the question as to how and why such well-schooled men should have strayed so far and so completely from the teaching of their childhood which embraced reverence for the biblical virtues of honesty, charity, and cleanliness of spirit. Did they completely forget those teachings? Were they no longer aware of moral values? There is a considerable difference in moral guilt between the criminal who does not know the meaning of honesty and the criminal who well understands the word and its significance but wilfully chooses to ignore its precepts.

There was thus at least this assurance in contemplating the Einsatzgruppen case, namely that since the defendants recalled episodes of past deeds of charity, kindness and God-fearing citizenship, they apparently still understood moral values.

On an occasion when the prosecution objected to the liberality with which I permitted the accused to introduce testimony on matters seemingly unassociated with the central issue, I ruled that in view of the serious pen-

246

alties which could accompany conviction, I would allow any evidence which could possibly have a bearing on mitigating the momentous accusations the defendants faced. I made only one exception. I would not permit any evidence on the social life of the penguins in the Antarctic. Later on I removed even that far-extending peripheral limitation and said that if defense counsel could show how such a subject could be relevant, we would listen to what they had to expound.

In time this assertion became known as the "Penguin Rule," and in enthusiastic appreciation of it the defendants presented scores of affidavits from people who had known them in their earlier years and attested to the proper and respectable lives they had previously led as civilians, the charitable acts they had performed, the merciful deeds they had accomplished, the civic obligations they had recognized, and the respectful regard they had displayed toward law and order. The material was quite revealing.

One listening to evidence in the Einsatzgruppen trial without adequate experience in the phenomena of what the human soul is capable of comprehending might well, at moments, have despaired of the human race. Here were crimes that defied language in the depth and vastness of their brutality. Here pitilessness reached its nadir and nothing in Dante's imagined Inferno could equal the horror of what we discovered happened in 1941, 1942 and 1943 in Poland, White Ruthenia, the Ukraine, Lithuania, Esthonia, Latvia, the Crimea, and western Russia. During the trial we were constantly being confronted with acts of man which defied every conceivable perspective of morality and conscience. We looked in on scenes of savage depravity on so unparalleled a scale that we recoiled as if from a blast of scalding steam.

247

But, even so, there was this extraordinary aspect of the case: The pages of the testimonials attesting to the former good character of many of the defendants fairly glittered with such phrases as "honest and truth-loving," "straight-thinking and friendly manner," "industrious, assiduous and good-natured," "of a sensitive nature," "absolutely honest." One could have doubted that they had ever even known the meaning of such words.

Piercing through the acrid smoke of the executing rifles, penetrating through the fumes of the gas vans, lifting the curtain of the unuttered last words of the one million slaughtered, the defendants did recall the precepts they had gained at their mothers' knee. Though they seemed not to perceive the monstrous contrast between the Einsatzgruppen deeds and the moral lessons of the distant past, yet they did recognize that the latter were still desirable. So long as even Einsatzgruppen assassins could appreciate the better rules of life, one should never regard hopelessly the future of man and his works.

In their final statements many of the defendants paid high tribute to the qualities of mercy and humaneness. This again called attention to the appalling moral abyss which yawned between the green-covered slopes of their youthful promise and the bleak cliffs of their adult degradation. Many of the affidavits spoke of religion. One affidavit introduced in behalf of Willy Seibert told how he often accompanied his mother to church. While in the Crimea exterminating human beings, did he recall these visits to the house of God, and if he did, could he reconcile his actions there with the teachings of religion and the tutelage of his mother?

Our court was a court of law so that the presence or absence of religious faith on the part of any defendant was not a subject for debate or even comment. The fact,

248

however, that Seibert advanced his early Christian training as an item of defense proclaimed that he at least recognized a dissimilarity between the books he studied as a
child and the pages on which he wrote with blood as a
man. This affidavit was additionally interesting because it
impliedly repudiated the denunciations of religion by
men like Bormann, Goebbels, Rosenberg, Himmler, and
above all, Hitler himself, who designated the church as
the only remaining unconquered ideological opponent of
National Socialism, continually insulting it in speeches
and pronounciamentos.

Reichsleiter Martin Bormann spoke for Hitler when he
said:

> National Socialist and Christian concepts are irrecon-
> cilable . . . If therefore in the future, our youth knows
> nothing more of this Christianity whose doctrines are far
> below ours, Christianity will disappear by itself . . . All
> influences which might impair or damage the leadership
> of the people exercised by the Fuehrer with the aid of the
> NSDAP must be eliminated. More and more people must
> be separated from the churches and their organs, the
> pastors.

Bormann had no difficulty in convincing the Einsatzgruppen leaders. Otto Rasch even anticipated Bormann.
This man, who spoke so feelingly of his tender regard for
young animals and of the devoutness of his parents, abandoned the church at the age of twenty-eight and soon
afterwards donned the brown shirt of Nazidom. Others
joined Hitler's ranks first and then concluded that the
church and National Socialism were incompatible. When
questioned as to their religious beliefs at the time of their
capture following the armistice, ten of the defendants
said they had formally broken away from the church, ten

249

described themselves as "Believers in God," two said they were "nondenominational." (A few of these assertions coincided in the same persons.) Not one asserted he was a churchgoer or lived up to the vows of a formal religion. Ernst Biberstein, of course, as an ordained ex-minister, was *sui generis*.

Eichmann, to whom all these men reported, had set the pattern when, years before, in joining the SS, he said that he did "not believe in religion."

It is not within the compass of these pages to discuss the moral and religious implications rising from the deeds and the lives of the performers of the Einsatzgruppen program. Religion, which through the ages, has strengthened the weak, aided the poor, and comforted the lonely and oppressed, is man's own determination, but that a minister of the gospel, via the road of Nazism, participated in mass executions, is a phenomenon that has its own implications. When the Swastika replaced the Cross, and *Mein Kampf* dislodged the Bible, it was inevitable that the German people were headed for disaster. When the Fuehrer-oath took the place of the Golden Rule, Truth was ousted and Falsehood enthroned to rule with an absolutism no monarch has ever known. Under the despotic regime of the lie, prejudice supplanted justice, arrogance canceled understanding, hatred superseded benevolence—and the columns of the Einsatzgruppen marched.

PART FIVE

The Verdict

CHAPTER NINETEEN

WHEN ALL THE EVIDENCE HAD BEEN PRESENTED, EACH defendant was offered the opportunity to address the Court orally, this in addition to the closing argument of his attorney. This privilege, not an Anglo-Saxon usage, was allowed because it conformed to European practice. Thus every defendant obtained the full benefits of an Anglo-Saxon trial, which gave him the witness chair from which to speak at length under the friendly questioning of his own counsel, (a procedure strange to European courts) and he enjoyed as well all guarantees vouchsafed the accused by continental standards.

Ohlendorf spoke first, holding the courtroom spellbound with a speech that would have done justice to a chair of philosophy at the University of Berlin. Erudite and profound, the discourse could have been addressed to students in history and political science and bore little resemblance to a plea for mercy, and certainly none for exoneration. While not exactly defending National Socialism, Ohlendorf said that those who were attracted to it "were longing for spiritual support, for a goal behind the social order into which they were born, a goal which promised them true human dignity, firm human objectives, and a spiritual and religious center for their development into human beings." He failed to tell us, however, how National Socialism was to achieve that goal, for, if there was one thing which National Socialism did not do, it was to promote respect for human dignity and a spiritual, religious development of human beings!

I was hoping Ohlendorf would talk longer, for his speech was very interesting if not very convincing, but after twenty minutes he suddenly concluded with a tribute to the Tribunal: "If the Tribunal please, I do not wish to end my final statement without expressing my gratitude for the very generous way in which you have dealt with the problems which we have regarded as important to these proceedings."

With the exception of Sandberger, Biberstein, Braune and Strauch, all the defendants availed themselves of that final word, and while their statements added little to the objectivity of the trial they illumined a little more the motivations behind the conduct which brought them before an international court to answer for what they had done. The defendants Yost, Naumann, Blume, Haensch, Klingelhoefer and Schubert, for instance, all declared that they had joined the Nazi Party and participated in its activities because of the menace of Bolshevism, but they offered no explanation as to why they remained with the Party when Hitler reduced their ardent beliefs to charred cinders by joining up with the very evil forces he had theretofore so bitterly denounced and castigated. The Nazi-Soviet pact transformed into mockery everything the Nazi hierarchy had said against Communism. The defendants had ample time after that revelation of monumental dishonesty and fraud to withdraw from the Nazi organizations they had voluntarily joined. Their con-

253

tinued adherence, therefore, to Hitler and Nazism revealed their steadfast approval of Hitler's aggressions and his persecution of unoffending, innocent peoples. Hitler's attack on Poland, with Stalin's formidable support, opened the gulf between good and evil, into which the defendants, with open eyes, walked to their own destruction.

With the taking of testimony and hearing of argument terminated, the defendants had been accorded not only every right laid down in the Charter agreed upon by the Allied nations, but those guaranteed under the Constitution of the United States and within the scope of the English common law. The defendants never knocked at the door of an additional privilege but that it was opened to them.

The trial ended, Judge Speight, Judge Dixon and I proceeded to review the record which contained 6,895 pages of testimony and 984 documents introduced on both sides. We met every day for three or four weeks to consider the factual and legal issues. We felt deeply the solemnity of our task, which involved not only passing on the lives and liberties of twenty-two men (Rasch having been severed from the case), but meeting as well the responsibility of justifying our action before the world. The final written Judgment in the case had to answer all doubts regarding this determined and objective affirmation of international law to hold individuals accountable to the law of nations and the law of humanity.

The Judgment also had to be a document which would serve notice on all future dictators and their compliant supporters as to what they could expect in the event they failed to heed the precedent of Nuremberg.

Not the least of the many purposes of the Nuremberg

trials was to give the German people an opportunity to perceive the real character of those who were their leaders and what they had done to bring Germany to its present state of ruin. That Hitler exercised practically limitless power is obvious, but he could never have brought down the walls of the twentieth century had he not found fanatic collaborators like the Einsatz defendants who accepted his mad outpourings and hysterical maledictions as if they were the pronouncements and apostrophes of a semidivinity. One or two of the defendants said that Hitler could not be resisted.

It is not true that Hitler could not be resisted. There were many who did resist him, or at least they refused to be party to his monstrous criminality. Many fled their native land with all its tender associations of school days, romance and roseate dreams, rather than accept him as their master. Others opposed him and were committed to concentration camps. It is error to assume that everyone in Germany approved of Nazism with the crimes it engendered. Had that been true, there would have been no need of the whip-slashing stormtroopers, the iron-heeled Gestapo, and the torture chamber.

Hitler struck the match, but the tiny blaze would have vanished swiftly had it not been for his fellow arsonists, big and small, who continued to supply the fuel until they, themselves, were enveloped by the fire they had been so fervently tending.

If history has taught anything it has demonstrated with devastating finality that most of the evils of the world have been due to craven subservience by subchiefs to one superchief whose plans, proposed by anyone else, would be rejected as mad. In his final statement to the Court at the end of the trial, the defendant Steimle admitted the supreme dereliction of abandoning the com-

255

pass of one's conscience to follow leaders who mark a course through the swamps of crime, the bogs of sin, and the quicksands of violence. "I will say this," remarked Steimle, "hundreds of thousands have, together with me, placed their faith and idealism into the hands of a few people with too great a confidence and have thereby laid the foundation of one of the causes of our unfortunate time."

CHAPTER TWENTY

AFTER SEVERAL WEEKS OF REVIEWING AND DELIBERATING ON the evidence, it became apparent that in the discharge of our solemn duty we would be required to impose the death sentence on some of the defendants.

This realization filled me with a sense of disquietude and sadness.

Throughout my ten years on the bench in my home state of Pennsylvania prior to the war, I was singularly fortunate in not having had to sentence anyone to the ultimate penalty. That duty, never easy for any judge, would have been particularly painful to me because of an instinctive aversion to violence in any form, reaching its extreme manifestation in the forcible extinguishing of human life. However, despite my tenderheartedness, if such it could be termed, I now found myself confronted with the possibility, if not probability, that I would be required to sentence not only one but many persons to an abrupt ending of their living days.

I felt I would need some spiritual restrengthening to prepare myself for the ordeal ahead. I conferred with Captain Francis B. Konieczny, the army chaplain at the

Nuremberg Military Post, and asked him if he could arrange for a retreat where I might dwell in meditation and prayer. He recommended the Cistercian Monastery in Seligenporten, some thirty miles distant from the Palace of Justice and its grim companion in stone, the prison, which held the men who were to receive the sentences the law was to impose.

At the monastery I was received by Father Abbot Stephan Geyer, who assigned me a small but comfortable room overlooking a beautiful garden. The monastery, which had been founded in the year 1215, was a perfect spot for seclusion and sanctuary and one in which to reflect on all I had heard and seen during the seven-months trial. Here I would prepare myself for the day whose events would become an inseparable part of my being and my everlasting memory.

To help me in any way I might need assistance, Father Abbot Stephan placed at my disposal Father Carlo Mesch who had studied in Rome and spoke fluent Italian. Although I had a smattering of the German language, I was not sufficiently equipped to carry on any prolonged conversation in it. Thus, Father Carlo became my interpreter in all my contacts with the German-speaking monks.

On my first day at the monastery, Father Carlo and I exchanged reminiscences on Rome, which he greatly admired and which had a tender spot in my affections because, as a youth, I had been a student at the University of Rome, and then I had participated in the campaign, which, under the command of General Clark, led to the liberation in 1944 of the Eternal City from the Nazi forces.

Each late afternoon, after strolling through the green

fields which surrounded the monastery and enjoying a cup of tea with the robed friars, I would retire to my room and listen enraptured to the organ music blossoming in the chapel and spreading its incense of harmony throughout the buildings and grounds, inundating my soul. One could not wish for a more tranquil and soothing environment.

During this period I received some additional moral reinforcements in the arrival of Lieutenant Giuseppe Ercolano, a comrade of war days, who came up from his home in Sorrento, where I had been military governor for a time, to offer his services. I found a unique task for him. During these awesome and soul-searching days I wished to keep myself apart from everybody but the gentle-visaged monks, my brother judges, and my office staff. Ercolano, good-natured and diplomatic, was able to fulfill this wish of mine.

For several days prior to the rendition of the Judgment I remained in the monastery wholly separated from the world of secular affairs. Then, on the morning of April 10, 1948, I took communion. Ercolano and Captain Konieczny, who had driven out from Nuremberg to attend the religious services, accompanied me to the Palace of Justice.

At ten o'clock the hundreds of people in the courtroom, which had been the scene of the sentencing to death of Goering, Ribbentrop, Jodl, Keitel, Sauckel and other leaders of the Nazi conspiracy, rose as Judge Speight, Judge Dixon and I entered and moved to our places on the bench while the marshal, Colonel Samuel L. Metcalfe, formally opened court. Straight ahead of us across the well of the room gaped the defendant's dock, empty as a schoolroom before the school bell rings, its emptiness accentuated by the throngs which filled all other spaces in the chamber, every face reflecting the nervous tension of anticipation.

On the day before, the Tribunal had announced the names of those who had been convicted and the counts of the indictment on which the convictions were based. The nature of the sentences, however, was locked in the bosoms of the judges. Now the convicted defendants were waiting in the basement of the building hard by the shaft of the elevator which was to take them, singly, to the fate awaiting them three floors above. By a very ingenious mechanism which had been installed by the Nazis themselves when they had meted out their brand of justice in this very chamber, the elevator carried the prisoner into the dock itself. A sliding panel in the wall served as the elevator door.

The attendants, guards, interpreters and lawyers now all being at their places, I announced, "The Marshal will produce the defendant Otto Ohlendorf." In a moment the elevator machinery began to turn. There followed a clicking of levers, a whirring of wheels, a hum of electrical energy being expended. The cage with its human freight was rising from the basement. Otto Ohlendorf, chief of Einsatzgruppen D, was on his way to receive his final orders.

The noise of the hoisting machinery ceased, the elevator door slid open without a sound, and Ohlendorf stepped forward into the dock. He bowed respectfully as he had been doing every court day for seven months, picked up the earphones, adjusted them precisely over his head, and then looked up at me expectantly with a clear, unafraid gaze.

"Otto Ohlendorf," I began, "you have been found

260

guilty on all counts which charged you with crimes against humanity, war crimes, and membership in criminal organizations. And—" Here I paused, for I had no intention of speaking rapidly. Ninety thousand murdered souls were perhaps listening; certainly the whole courtroom was listening and through the ears and eyes of those people the world was awaiting the tidings which would help to make life more sacred and secure in the future. "—the Court sentences you to death by hanging."

Ohlendorf's expression did not change. Actually, the slightest suggestion of a smile came to his lips, not a cynical smile, not a resentful smile, never a sneer—just an intellectual appreciation of what was happening, the inevitable which he had undoubtedly expected. Unembarrassed and unruffled, he removed his earphones, politely handed them to the guard by his side, and stepped back into the elevator, his shoulders still thrown back, his head still erect, the slight smile not fading.

The door murmured shut and Ohlendorf disappeared as if he had already dropped in the gallows. Only the whisperings of the turning wheels in the shaft were heard in the courtroom which was a vast, hushed chamber in which no one breathed, spoke, or stirred. A pause followed of even profounder quietude.

Then again was heard the soft hum of the elevator machinery and once more the door of fate was moving. This time Heinz Jost of slight build, deep-set eyes, and complete self-possession appeared. He stepped forward into the bright lights of the fluorescent chandeliers, picked up and adjusted his earphones, and looked forward to the bench expectantly. Only a few seconds were needed for his sentence.

"Heinz Jost, under the counts of the indictment of

261

which you have been found guilty, the Tribunal sentences you to life imprisonment."

The defendant bowed low and came to an erect position again, his expression lighted as if he had heard the Court say, "You are hereby notified that you are going on a luxury tour around the world." Perhaps the penalty of life imprisonment instead of death had brought him such relief that anything less than the rope seemed indeed a boon and a consummation devoutly to be enjoyed. Although as leader of Einsatzgruppen A he authorized executions, it was established in his behalf that he did at a certain time try to sabotage the Fuehrer-Order and he was allowed credit for this belated reformation.

I now turned the microphone over to Judge Speight, who in turn sentenced Erich Naumann to death by hanging and Erwin Schulz to twenty years' imprisonment. Judge Dixon then sentenced Franz Six to twenty years' imprisonment and Paul Blobel to death by hanging. I again took the microphone to sentence both Walter Blume and Martin Sandberger to death by hanging. Alternating after every two defendants, three of us imposed twenty-one sentences. Matthias Graf had been released.

As the elevator ascended and descended like the perpendicular swinging of the pendulum of fate, all the defendants, with the exception of two, took their medicine without a whimper. Facing the Tribunal bravely, erectly, uncomplainingly, they accepted their doom apparently just as readily as they had executed the orders which sent one million of their fellow men into eternity. Werner Braune was so much at ease that he did not bother to clamp the headphone over his head. He picked up the device and held it to one ear as one answers a telephone call. And then when he got the message that he was to die by hanging, he put down the instrument, seemingly to say, "Well, that's done."

The ex-minister Ernst Biberstein refused to look at the Tribunal or anyone in the courtroom. As he stepped out of the elevator, he tilted his head upward as if prepared to read his sentence on the ceiling. Nor did he change his posture or expression throughout the entire fateful proceeding. His demeanor did not seem to differ from the one he wore as he himself described it in witnessing the execution of women and children he had sentenced. When the words "death by hanging" had been translated into *Tod am Galgen,* and had fallen into his earphones, he stepped back without once modifying his glance, as though he would now read the remainder of the story through the roof of the elevator.

The defendant Eduard Strauch was somewhat less heroic in the courtroom than he had been in the execution ditches where, at times, he ordered the extraction of gold teeth from the mouths of his victims prior to killing them. On the two days immediately preceding the day of sentence, he had listened to the reading of the Judgment without manifesting any unusual symptoms, but, returned to his cell, he had spoken ramblingly to the guards. A board of doctors had again examined him and again found nothing abnormal in his mental state. Now he stood before us convinced that subterfuge was useless and he was sentenced to hang for the hideous crimes of which, in a happier day for him, he had boasted.

At 11:15 Strauch disappeared as Ohlendorf had disappeared an hour before. The other sentences were as follows:

WILLY SEIBERT	Death by hanging
EUGEN STEIMLE	Death by hanging
WALTER HAENSCH	Death by hanging
GUSTAV NOSSKE	Life imprisonment
ADOLF OTT	Death by hanging
WALDEMAR KLINGELHOEFER	Death by hanging
LOTHAR FENDLER	10 years' imprisonment
WALDEMAR VON RADETZKY	20 years' imprisonment
FELIX RUEHL	10 years' imprisonment
HEINZ SCHUBERT	Death by hanging

All the sentenced defendants except Nosske appealed to General Clay, the Military Governor, for mitigation or reduction of sentence. In March, 1949, General Clay affirmed all penalties. Later a Clemency Board reviewed the sentences and in January, 1951, some modifications were recommended and approved by John J. McCloy, United States High Commissioner for Germany.

Commissioner McCloy affirmed the death sentences of Ohlendorf, Naumann, Blobel and Braune. Strauch was extradited to Belgium for trial by the Belgian authorities for crimes committed there and he was there again sentenced to death. McCloy commuted to life imprisonment or a term of years the death penalties of Blume, Sandberger, Seibert, Steimle, Biberstein, Haensch, Ott, Klingelhoefer and Schubert. Radetzky and Ruehl were released on the time they had already served. Jost's term was reduced to ten years, Schulz's to fifteen years, Six's to ten years, Nosske's to ten years and Fendler's to eight years.

On June 8, 1951, Otto Ohlendorf, Erich Naumann, Paul Blobel and Werner Braune, together with Oswald Pohl, the head of the concentration camp system, and on whose trial I had also sat, were hanged at the Landsberg prison.

It was in this same Landsberg prison, in the Lech Val-

264

ley some fifty miles from Munich, that Adolf Hitler, twenty-four years before, had prepared the chart of the Nazi movement in his book *Mein Kampf*. Here he had declared that he was to be the "exclusive leader of the movement." He had no difficulty in finding those who were willing to accept him as that exclusive leader because they knew that in the aggressive, despoiling campaigns to be waged there would be booty and spoils for them also. There was, of course, nothing new in this program. Down through the ages there have always been Einsatz leaders, who, for personal enrichment and egotistical adornment, supported their Fuehrers, without regard to conscience, in aggressions over other peoples. The final result, however, has always been the same.

The theme of might against right has inevitably led to consequences which were eventually catastrophic to those who assumed themselves invincible. Through the pauseless sweep of the centuries, despots and tyrants have ever and again appealed to the cupidity of their subordinate commanders and have utilized the primitive vanity and arrogance of these little leaders in the accomplishment of their titanic horrors. Over and over, this monotonous and savage drama has appeared on the stage of history, but never was it played with such totality, fury and brutality as it was with the Nazis in the title role.

That so much man-made misery should have happened in the twentieth century, which could well have been the fruition of all the aspirations and hopes of the centuries which went before, made the spectacle of 1945 almost insupportable in its unutterable tragedy and sadness. Though most of the Einsatz defendants sought to rationalize their course of actions, it is possible they finally understood the disservice they rendered not only to humanity but to their own fatherland. It may even be that through the Einsatzgruppen trial with its horrifying revelations they accomplished the unintended benefit of demonstrating what are the inevitable consequences that attend any plan stemming from arrogance, hatred and intolerance. And there they may have proved what has never been disproved: There is only one fuehrer, and that is Truth.

SOURCE OF MATERIAL

Of course, most of the material in this book was taken from the daily transcript of the Einsatzgruppen trial and from memoranda and notebooks kept by myself throughout the trial. Copies of the transcript, mimeographed in English and German, may be found in the National Archives in Washington, the Library of Congress, the Library of the Harvard Law School, and in the Nuremberg State Archives at Nuremberg.

In addition to the bilingual transcripts, copies have been preserved, also in English and German, of all documents introduced in the trial, as well as many documents which were collected but not offered in evidence. One each of these "sets" (the transcript being in English) was deposited in the following libraries: University of California, University of Chicago, Columbia Law School, Duke University, Harvard Law School, the Hoover Institute (Stanford University), New York Public Library, University of North Dakota, Northwestern University, Princeton, University of Michigan, University of Western Law School, West Point, and the University of Wisconsin. Such sets are also on the shelves of the Wiener

Library in London and of the library of the United Nations. Additional sets (the transcript of the proceedings being in German) were sent to the Universities of Erlangen, Freibourg, Frankfurt, Goettingen, and Heidelberg, as well as to the State Chancellery at Munich.

In abbreviated form, the Einsatzgruppen trial, with documents, briefs, and testimony, was published by the United States Government in Volume IV of a series entitled *Trial of War Criminals*. The volumes may be purchased from the United States Government Printing Office and may be consulted in most large libraries.

The proceedings before the International Military Tribunal were published in forty-two volumes and are also available in the large libraries.

Most of the unusually important documents taken from Nazi sources were compiled and printed by the United States Government Printing Office in a series of volumes entitled *Nazi Conspiracy and Aggression*.

M. A. M.

ABOUT THE AUTHOR

As author of ten books, two of which (BLACK FURY and TEN DAYS TO DIE) were made into motion pictures, and presiding judge at the Nuremberg trial of twenty-three squad leaders who were responsible for the deaths of a million defenseless men, women and children, Judge Michael A. Musmanno is eminently qualified to write the story of the Eichmann kommandos.

He writes with the verve of one who has experienced danger and has lived through many dramatic events. As a naval officer during World War II, he was twice wounded in action, and a ship which he commanded was sunk by German bombs. He served for a time as military governor of the Sorrentine Peninsula in Italy, and during the latter phase of the war was naval aide to General Mark W. Clark. He was decorated with the Bronze Star for Valor, Legion of Merit, Purple Heart (with cluster), and the Military Order for Italy.

Following the war, General Clark assigned him to the presidency of the United States Forcible Repatriation Board in Austria which passed on the Soviet Union's demands for the return of Russian refugees. Musmanno saved some five thousand of these refugees from Siberia and the execution squad.

Before becoming a judge, Musmanno, in his home state of Pennsylvania, served in the Legislature for two years. He is an able speaker and has publicly debated with many personages, including the famous Clarence Darrow.

CPSIA information can be obtained at www.ICGtesting.com
Printed in the USA
BVOW05s1428070314

347010BV00009B/116/P